GLOBALISING HATRED

GLOBALISING HATRED

THE NEW ANTISEMITISM

DENIS MacSHANE

Weidenfeld & Nicolson
LONDON

First published in Great Britain in 2008
by Weidenfeld & Nicolson

1 3 5 7 9 10 8 6 4 2

© Denis MacShane 2008

A CIP catalogue record for this book
is available from the British Library.

ISBN: 978 0 297 84473 0

Typeset at The Spartan Press Ltd,
Lymington, Hants

Printed and bound at CPI Mackays,
Chatham ME5 8TD

The Orion Publishing Group's policy is to use papers that
are natural, renewable and recyclable products and made
from wood grown in sustainable forests. The logging and
manufacturing processes are expected to conform to the
environmental regulations of the country of origin.

Weidenfeld & Nicolson

The Orion Publishing Group Ltd
Orion House
5 Upper Saint Martin's Lane
London, WC2H 9EA
An Hachette Livre UK Company

www.orionbooks.co.uk

Contents

Preface

I have written this short book because I see the profound dangers of a vicious and destructive ideology that has crept into our body politic and social. 'Antisemitism cannot be banned', writes Frederic Raphael, 'yet, it seems, it would be grotesque not to challenge it.' This is my personal challenge. Raphael, who describes himself as a non-religious Jew, was writing in 1997. 'My experience of antisemitism has never been life-threatening', he writes. In the decade since he wrote those complacent words we have seen life-threatening antisemitism return with a vengeance. Thousands have been killed across the globe as men, women, even children and organisations powered by an ideology to which antisemitism is central and essential have decided to unleash unprecedented assaults on democracy. In Bali and Istanbul, in Egypt and Madrid, in New York and London, people driven by antisemitic hate along with other hates have killed, killed and killed again in the name of a cause that hates Jews.

That antisemitic hate now kills more Muslims than Jews is one of the unintended consequences that history relishes. Readers who want a calm, dispassionate current affairs essay should stop now. I have written a book that I hope is polemical, partisan and political. There are many factual, historical accounts on antisemitism that I list in the Select Bibliography. At last count there were more than 40,000 published works on antisemitism. Among them is *Antisemitism: A Very Short Introduction* published in 2007 in the fine Oxford University Press series. The author writes of a 'nosological approach to antisemitism' and tells us 'Individuals of Jewish descent growing up in this antisemitically informed discourse supposedly internalized the antisemitic image of the Jews' with much more of this rarefied academic language. He concludes with the assertion that 'the answer to antisemitism is ultimately not a Jewish state, but the establishment of a truly global system of liberal pluralism'. How can I as a European progressive object to global liberal pluralism? Between today and arriving at that nirvana there are one or two obstacles. One of them is global neo-antisemitism, the development of an old hate into an organised ideology with its thinkers, organisers, spokespersons, state sponsors and millions of adherents. Today's neo-antisemitism is not about Jews. It is about us.

So this book is not addressed exclusively to Jews. It is written for the vast majority of people in my country, my continent, my world that have no idea that antisemitism is back with a deadly vengeance. I refer to neo-antisemitism because although the hates are old, neo-antisemitism is a twenty-first-century global ideology that has to be understood in political terms if it is to be confronted and contained. I am a Member of Parliament representing people of different origins and different beliefs in my working-class, South Yorkshire constituency. Jews in Britain and across the world are right to be concerned about the return of antisemitism as a serious political phenomenon.

Organised neo-antisemitism is like a rat in our entrails preventing just and equitable solutions to key world problems and replacing hope with hate. Combating neo-antisemitism should now be a major political priority for progressive politics. I am neither Jewish nor does the politics of 'Israel, right or wrong' make any sense to me. But I have spent my political life fighting racism, intolerance, hate and denial of a people's or a state's right to exist. I am intolerant of intolerance. There is no greater intolerance today than neo-antisemitism in all its open and disguised, witting and unwitting forms. I do not expect to change the mind of those who believe the truth has been revealed on these questions. I would like to create a politics of anti-antisemitism and a politics that allows all European Muslims to become fully European without denying their faith. The book is also an appeal for a return to rationality and international law as guidelines in global politics.

In the summer of 2005 I put together a commission of senior parliamentarians to create the first-ever All-Party Parliamentary Commission of Inquiry to look into the problem of antisemitism. The MPs included the former leader of the Conservative Party, Iain Duncan Smith, and the senior Liberal MP Chris Huhne. Former ministers took part as well as distinguished former and present chairmen of Parliamentary Select Committees. Lady Sylvia Hermon MP represented the Ulster Unionists and Khalid Mahmood, one of Britain's first Muslim MPs, also served on the commission.

Our report was published in 2006. The government's response to it, in the unusual form of a Command Paper, was published in 2007. None of the commission's members were Jewish. None had taken much active part in the passionate Commons debates on Israel and Palestine. I had only made a brief visit to Israel twenty-five years ago and other than a general interest linked to my work as Europe minister and continuing interest in foreign affairs I do not consider myself to be an expert on Israel. The commission's work could not avoid the question of Israel however. Neo-antisemitism is inextricably linked to the Middle East imbroglio.

For the avoidance of doubt as lawyers say, my position would be that Israel has to make a settlement along the lines of its territories as they stood in 1967. Jerusalem remains a contentious issue. As someone baptised and brought up a Catholic, the notion that the city in which Christ was crucified is not part of the Christian heritage or should be under the control of just one of the three Abrahamic monotheisms cannot make sense. If and when a Palestinian state is created, its capital will be in an east Jerusalem open and accessible to all.

This book is not about religion, though it is impossible to discuss Jew-hatred and antisemitism without reference to religion. There are plenty of book by Jews on the problem or on the question of Israel, which are written from a more knowledgeable basis of Judaism and the two other Abrahamic faiths than I can ever hope to acquire. As I tell my 10,000 Muslim constituents when I talk in their mosques, in their homes, or in political discussion with those who are with me in the Labour Party, Islam the faith is not the issue. It is Islamism the ideology that must be discussed openly and when it supports antisemitism or the denial of democracy and human rights it must be opposed. The Tunisian-born French Muslim intellectual Abdelwahab Meddeb, in a book written in 2008, argues that:

Islam will not arrive at an acceptable solution to its problems as long as it wants to place the question of politics – issues of law and the state – as an absolute because it then makes the question impossible to answer. Thanks to the separation of politics and religion, the entire process of thought and western history has consisted of the successful separation of law from that impossible absolute.

Meddeb goes on to describe 'the sickness of Islamism which extends even to legitimising crime'. In a moving section of this book he describes how Muslim families in wartime Tunisia protected Jews from both German Nazis and French collaborators. Thus antisemitism is not born of Islam or in the DNA of Muslims.

It is Islamism the ideology that has unleashed new twenty-first-century antisemitism and it is impossible to discuss the problem without dealing with Islamism. Jason Burke, one of our clearest writers on the recent politics of the region and on Al-Qaeda, prefers the term 'modern Islamic militancy'. Joschka Fischer, the best foreign minister Europe has seen in recent years, talks of the 'new totalitarianism of jihadi fundamentalism'. In April 2008, the Council of Europe, representing forty-seven European nations, adopted a policy declaration that argued 'against any confusion between Islam as a faith and Islamic fundamentalism as an ideology'. Gilles Kepel, the leading French Arabist and expert on Islamism, writes of 'anti-western Islamist reasoning' sinking roots in Britain. Islamist and Islamism are terms used by political scientists examining Islamic politics but they remain useful as an adjective and noun, different to the religion, Islam, and the believer, a Muslim. I have spent much of my political life working with Muslims in different countries and now represent many Muslims in my constituency. They are people of peace, proud of family, faith and their attachment to Kashmir, Yemen and other places they or their forefathers came from. Their future requires the defeat of antisemitism.

As long as antisemitism is allowed its place in politics the great cause of peace in the Middle East will never be realised.

The Nobel Laureate Amartya Sen argues that 'Central to leading a human life . . . are the responsibilities of choice and reasoning. In contrast, violence is promoted by the cultivation of inevitability about some allegedly unique – often belligerent – identity that we are supposed to have and which apparently makes extensive demands on us (sometimes of a most disagreeable kind).' Global neo-antisemitism is part of the chain of arguments that insists on the 'unique identity' of Jews and Jewishness, which in the view of the antisemites can only be combated by forms of violence, verbal or physical, initiated by intellectuals, states as well as political organisations.

If just a handful are persuaded by the arguments in this book and one or two people slink away in shame as they realise how remarks and writings feed this new-old evil, the book will have served its purpose.

Denis MacShane

August 2008

Introduction

When I first began political activity in the 1970s, anti-semitism seemed to belong to the history books. I was brought up a Catholic and I suppose the first Jews I met would have been at Oxford. Even there, I was Jew-blind so to speak and only learnt that a friend or fellow student-journalist was Jewish because someone drew it to my attention. A good friend then and now was Jonathon Green, the lexicographer. Only much later did I come to realise he was Jewish. On a train to the Labour Party conference in Bourne-mouth in September 2007 I was talking to Robert Peston, the BBC's economic correspondent and someone whose political and economic journalism I have long admired. I told him I was working on this book and he said he was Jewish. Again, I had no idea. Put it down to naivety but as with the close political work I undertake with Muslim councillors and political activists in my Yorkshire constituency I simply stop seeing people in terms of skin colour or religion.

And yet, and yet. Antisemitism is always there. The prominent American political commentator Ann Coulter de-clares on television that Jews need 'to be perfected'. As I write, the sports pages have been gripped by the fact that the rich Russian, Roman Abramovich, who owns Chelsea is Jewish and the manager he appointed to run the team is Israeli. The *Daily Mail* seemed to think the most important news to lead its back-page sports coverage was that both men would celebrate the Jewish holy day of Yom Kippur. (What did the *Mail* expect them to do, attend mass?) The club's chairman was moved to write in the Chelsea programme that the antisemitic letters and emails the club were receiving were unacceptable. When Chelsea played Manchester United, the *Daily Telegraph* reported, Chelsea fans sang a song to the well-known football crowd melody 'We're on our way to Wembley' replacing it with the words, 'Roman is on his way to Auschwitz – Hitler's going to gas him again.' At the same time in Prague, the Czech TV channel CT had to shut down the chants of fans from the Sparta club who screamed '*Jude*' – 'Jews' – at their city rival team, Slavia. In an earlier match, August 2007, the Czech football association fined the international player Pavel Horvath 7,000 euros for repeatedly raising his right arm in a Nazi salute during a match.

Meanwhile, in New York Iranian president Mahmoud Ahmadinejad told students at Columbia University that he stood by his view that the Holocaust was a lie. In India, a company launched a new line in bedspreads called the 'Nazi Collection' for rich Indians to go to bed under. When challenged by India's 5,000-strong Jewish community, the firm's owner said Nazi stood for 'New Arrival Zone for India' and was not meant to be antisemitic. Of course.

In England, David Irving was boasting to *The Guardian* newspaper that he was back in business speaking and writing antisemitic tosh. Irving had been sentenced by an Austrian court in 2005 after referring to the gas chambers at Auschwitz as a 'fairy tale'. Under Austrian and German law, denying the Holocaust (and thus whitewashing Hitler) is taken rather more seriously than in Britain or America. Irving was released after appealing to a higher Austrian court, which let him go saying that Irving had undergone an 'impeccable conversion' from his early antisemitic views. Not quite. Talking to *The Guardian*, Irving said that his views on the Holocaust have crystallised rather than changed. He says that he believes the Jews were responsible for what happened to them during the Second World War and that the 'Jewish problem' was responsible for nearly all of the wars of the past 100 years: 'The Jews are the architects of their own misfortune,' he declared.

In the 1990s, Irving was a favourite of the BBC and other television programmes. The Conservative politician Alan Clark attended a book launch for one of Irving's three biographies of Hitler where guests mixed their drinks with cocktail sticks adorned with a Nazi flag. At the event Irving produced this couplet, read out at one of the many trials his antisemitic views have prompted:

> I am a Baby Aryan,
> Not Jewish or sectarian,
> I have no plans to marry,
> An Ape or Rastafarian.

Irving is an old man now, nearly 70, but antisemitism never seems to grow old. One of the oldest of the antisemitic tropes is that of the lobby, or network, or cabal of Jews in high places who have disproportionate influence over political, economic or media decisions. As I read despairingly about Chelsea and Sparta fans, about Irving and Ahmadinejad, I go into a bookshop in Paris and there is a French translation of a book by two American professors claiming to reveal that American foreign policy is controlled by Jews. Then I travel to Iceland for a conference and in a bookshop in Reykjavik I find the same book about the secret power of the Jews on sale. There is no corner of the globe free of the core antisemitic myth of the Jewish lobby and its conspirational networks and hidden influence and powers. Sweden's equivalent of Britain's left weekly, the *New Statesman*, is called *Ordfront Magasin*. In 2005, an article was published with the heading 'Swedish media is controlled by the Israeli regime'. The journalist, Johannes Wahlström, said — wait for it — a secret 'lobby' in Sweden stopped any criticism of Israel in the country's media. Sweden has the most openly anti-Israel journalism, from the left and the right, of any Western democracy. But use the magic words, 'secret' and 'lobby', and all judgement leaves an editor's or publisher's desk. In November 2007, Algeria's Minister for Veteran Affairs, Mohammed Cherif Abbas, blamed the Jewish lobby in France for the arrival of President Nicolas Sarkozy, who has some Jewish blood, as head of the French state.

> You know the origins of the French president and those who put him into power. Do you know that the Israelis printed a stamp with Nicolas Sarkozy on it during the election campaign? . . . Why has Bernard Kouchner [a non-believing Jew who was a Socialist minister and accepted Sarkozy's invitation to become foreign minister] decided to cross the floor? It's the result of a movement that reflects the views of the real architects of Sarkozy's arrival in power — the Jewish lobby.

Ah, the lobby again. And so the antisemitic story goes on.

I cannot hope to persuade the Irvings, Chelsea and Sparta fans, the Islamists, Algeria's Minister Abbas or the Iranians who want to wipe Israel off the world map that their antisemitism is wrong. We live in a world in which intolerant politics is profitable in terms of profile and votes. And it is no exaggeration to say that antisemitism has become something of an industry. Racism is its core, but it is also part of the new politics of contempt for the other, something far more than crude, knuckle-headed prejudice. The anti-racist movements in Britain or the civil rights movements in the United States have changed politics and law. Jews in Britain enjoy civic rights. But too many of them, especially observant religious Jews, live with the discomfort of an anti-Jewish discourse in mainstream politics and the media as well as direct physical attacks on their children, their religious buildings and cemeteries, not even finding peace in death. The Panglossian argument is made by American-based professors like Tony Judt and John Mearsheimer that there really isn't, after all, much antisemitism in Europe. They cite opinion polls and helpfully point out that the state-organised antisemitism of Russian pogroms or right-wing nationalist politics of the 1920s and 1930s is not happening again. The latter point is true, but there are new dark clouds that need monitoring and combating. When, in France, a poor Jew is kidnapped, tortured and killed because his assailants said they knew Jews were rich and had money to pay for his release, we should be concerned. When a man is killed in Paris as he is caught up in a wave of anti-Jewish violence after a football game, alarm bells should ring. And when at a London football match the crowd chants: 'I'd rather be a Paki than a Jew', we should do more than just note it. Perhaps we need to learn from the US civil rights movement. Just as antisemitism has not been eradicated in Europe, racism has not been killed in Louisiana. While there is no longer the scale of deep-south US racism that the civil rights movement marched against in the 1950s and 1960s, the movement has not gone to sleep. When small African-American children are harassed and intimidated in Louisiana, American anti-racists take to the streets again. They know the racist snake has been scotched, but not killed. Where are Europe's anti-antisemites when they are needed?

Of course, political antisemitism is on the fringe of politics. But for the first time in post-war European history, an organised block of parliamentarians from different countries was formed in 2007 in the European Parliament despite their antisemitic views. That it later collapsed, as the hates between antisemites and ultra-nationalists are usually greater than any unity they can sustain, is some consolation. Britain's BNP and France's *Front National* also suffer from fissures. The vast majority of British citizens repudiate antisemitism and believe along with the American professors that it hardly exists. Yet the independent parliamentary report produced by senior British MPs for the House of Commons concluded that too many British Jews lived with a level of fear, anxiety and concern about their Jewishness that was not acceptable. To the American academics anxious to make their points about Jewish power and influence in America, the fact that British Jews do worry about antisemitism may seem of little importance.

British thinking on racist incidents, including antisemitic assaults and intimidation, has changed following the report by Sir William McPherson into the murder of a young black boy, Stephen Lawrence, in south London in 1995. McPherson argued that it was the victim rather than the perpetrator of a racist insult or attack who should define whether or not it was racist (or antisemitic). This, it may be argued, allows too much subjective interpretation by the person who has been insulted or attacked. The individual may protest: 'I am not antisemitic I just don't like the way Jews behave, or their support for Israel, or the money they have, or the top jobs they get in the professions or the media, or their irritating demands not to work or do exams on Saturdays.' After McPherson, however, it is now the victim of antisemitism who decides what is or what is not antisemitic. The right-wing Jew-baiter, the Islamist Jew-hater or all those liberal-leftists who proclaim they are not antisemitic but who deny Jews their Jewishness in the full sense of being Jewish, including their affection for the one state in the world where antisemitism by definition cannot exist, now have to come to terms with antisemitism being what Jews feel and say it is.

McPherson has set a higher bar and many may argue that it is too high and too protective of Jews, especially when it comes to the question of Israel and Palestine. The Old Etonian doyen of leftist intellectualism in Britain is Perry Anderson. He speaks for many of his class, generation and the effortless superiority of the *bien pensant* English intellectual when he describes in the *London Review of Books* (where else?) Middle East 'terrorism' as 'armed resistance' and the elected Palestinian Authority-government as 'a remnant valet in the West Bank'. It is not clear whether in the Andersonian world view the dead of London of 7/7 or the greater number of dead in the 11 March 2004 Madrid attack are also victims of 'armed resistance', but since the new *trahison des clercs* is to blame democracy and excuse terrorism we should not wait for an answer.

What's taking shape is a subtle encouragement just to muddle along, being watchful of any overt antisemitism and cracking down hard when it arises, but otherwise dismissing antisemitism as not important as a contemporary problem, or saying, as many do, that the issue of antisemitism is simply cranked up by pro-Israel propagandists who seek to deflect any criticism of Israel by branding it as antisemitic. And then I read that Oxford University Vice-Chancellor Dr John Hood had 'cast doubts' on one of the key planks of government policy: tracking and rooting out antisemitic activists in extremist Islamist organisations on campus. One of the few followers of antisemitic politics is the writer Ed Husain. He has described how together with fellow radical Islamist ideologues he turned his campus into a centre of antisemitic hate. And he notes that what astonished his group was that the campus authorities did nothing to stop the spread of antisemitism. That was in the 1990s. Oxford's Dr Hood shows that little has changed. The complacency and the refusal to challenge and defeat the antisemitism of Islamist extremism is still alive even at the price of Jewish university students not enjoying their right to live on a campus free of fear and hate. Of course, the good Dr Hood dressed up his point of view by saying that tackling extremism 'had potentially serious consequences for academic freedom and free speech' but rather missed the point that the neo-antisemitism of campus Islamist extremism is all about denying freedom to Jews (or for that matter to gays and to women who want to control their own lives rather than be controlled by patriarchal clerisy). Little wonder that David Irving had a free run at British universities over a number of years as the principle of free speech was extended to those who support the politics that would deny all freedoms to Jews. Little wonder that soon after the doubts of Oxford University's vice-chancellor about working with the public authorities to expose Jew-hating extremism on the campus, David Irving (along with the BNP's Nick Griffin) was invited to speak by the public-school-educated gentlemen of the Oxford Union. The National Union of Students, which is a lot more aware of reactionary extreme Islamist antisemitism and the hurt it does to Jewish students, plays a different role. It has a policy of 'No Platform' for antisemitic organisations and their insults and assaults on Jewish students.

After an attack in Paris on a sunny Saturday in June 2008 by a group armed with iron bars left a young Jew wearing his kippa in a coma, the French Union of Jewish Students expressed concern that fewer and fewer Jewish students seek entry into universities in France as they fear they will be made uncomfortable by anti-Jewish remarks or by hostility to the beliefs and causes supported by young French Jews. In July 2008 it was reported that the number of antisemitic incidents on British university campuses had almost doubled compared with the previous year. Again, those lecturers and activists who denounce Jewish causes will proclaim that they are not antisemitic, yet, bit by bit, the creation of a university space in today's Europe which is *judenfrei* – free of Jews – can be seen to come into being.

So today's antisemitism is not just traditional Jew-hatred, nor can it be reduced to a variant of racism. It is a growing component element of international politics. Antisemitism is exported by a number of states and has an impact on geopolitics that should not be underestimated. It is part of the new anti-Occidentalism, a denial of the values that arose following the Renaissance and Reformation, that were given full philosophical and political meaning in the Enlightenment years and that have been the guiding politics of all democratic and human rights international campaigning since the middle of the last century and the creation of the United Nations. Today's state-supported antisemitism is a reversion to the politics of the sixteenth and seventeenth centuries before the Treaty of Westphalia in 1648. The break-up of a single Christianity in the sixteenth century saw religious difference define interstate relations. Catholics fought Protestants and vice versa, each believing they had the right to impose their religious ideas beyond their own state borders. This clash of Christian civilisations culminated in the Thirty Year War, which devastated continental Europe in the first half of the seventeenth century. It was ended with the peace of Westphalia. The principle was established of *Cuius regio, eius religio*, namely that the religion of the king would be the religion of the nation, but kings would not seek to impose their religious beliefs on other states.

The Westphalian system was challenged by revolutionary moments as in 1789 and in 1917 when one nation believed it had discovered the single luminous truth and had the right to export or impose it on other countries. In a modified form the Westphalian system is also under challenge from liberal or neo-conservative interventionists, and the debate about when intervention – whether in the Balkans, in Africa, in Afghanistan and other parts of the worlds – is justified occupies serious thinkers on international policy. However, the general Westphalian rule of non-interference, non-export of religious politics and respect for the sovereign statehood of UN members still holds good. With one flagrant exception. The Kingdom of Saudi Arabia arrogates to itself, with all the passion of a Catholic monarchy seeking to destroy heretic Protestants or vice versa, the right to export antisemitism within the framework of its Wahhabist fundamentalism version of Islam. Never has so much money been spent to support a version of a religion that is so hostile to Jews and to the Jewish state. But state-sanctioned antisemitism is not exclusive to Saudi Arabia. The government and rulers of Iran also defy the interstate norms as laid down by the Westphalian principles by a high-level endorsement of core antisemitic politics including calls for Israel to disappear and support for Jew-hating Holocaust denial. From the first days of Israel's existence, states like Nasser's Egypt called up all the demons of nineteenth- and twentieth-century European antisemitism as part of official state ideology.

Today, however, it is Saudi Wahhabism that is the most developed form of organised antisemitism and it is no

accident that the most dedicated opponent and willing mur-
derer of Jews and the citizens of any country that does not
subscribe to antisemitic hatred is the Saudi Osama Bin Laden.
The dependence of the US and other advanced economies on
Saudi and Gulf oil means that the violation of the Westphalian system and the export of religious intolerance and
hate by Saudi Wahhabism is not challenged by any US
president or European leader. There is little respect for
human rights as universally defined and recognised in Saudi
Arabia or Iran. But as long as the cruelties and denial of
human rights were confined to the Wahhabist Sunni kingdom of the Saudis or to the Shia theocracy of Iran it could be
argued that the religious rules enforced there were the internal matter of the two states. But in the last quarter of a
century there has been a growing export of religious intolerance as well as financial and political support for violent
groups willing to transform religious hate into suicide bombs,
sending women and children to die in the name of Jew-
hatred. And, as demonstrated by the fifteen Saudi citizens
who were on the planes that caused carnage in New York on
9/11, in many parts of Europe and Asia, Saudi money pays for
the training of men who will then be sent to preach the un-
forgiving Wahhabi belief systems to gullible targets within
the Muslim community. Much Islam is an appeal for tolerance
and coexistence between the faiths and peoples of 'the Book',
namely Muslims, Christians and Jews. This is not the case of
Wahhabism.

Thus antisemitism has many different facets. It is both an
expression of racism and yet also has deep religious roots. It
is social and appeals to intellectuals who look for networks
and secret influence to explain state policy. It is international.
With just a smear of make-up, antisemites can hide behind
appeals to populism, or nationalism, or to solidarity with third-

world struggle. It is state-sanctioned. It is exported by states. Modern antisemitism is multi-dimensional. Antisemitism was once called the socialism of fools. It is now the ideology of clever and determined men, with limitless amounts of money and important state power behind them. It is both the smash on the head of a rabbi walking home in north London and the push on a button that blows people to oblivion on a London underground train a few kilometres away. Today, it is the world's most pernicious ideology and practice, international in its reach and capable of taking different forms from the university campus to the upper-class dinner party. It ranges from the Jewish-influence conspiracy theories to the suicide bomber educated into a hatred of Jews as well as a hatred for the democratic states that will not permit a genocide of Jews to happen again.

Israel also has its supporters in the Commons. Many of them are Jewish MPs, though the Jewish Labour MP Sir Gerald Kaufman is vehement in his denunciation of Israeli policy he disagrees with. Everyone, it seems, has a view on the Israel-Palestine conflict and how to solve it. There are ultras in both camps who will accept nothing less than the effective end to a Jewish state. On the other hand, there are those who believe that Palestinians should go and become Jordanian citizens and let Israel annexe the land occupied after 1967.

Language can be found in both the Palestinian and Israeli camps that can support either position. When the United Nations authorised the use of armed force to restore the integrity of UN member Kuwait following its 1991 invasion and occupation by Iraq, Palestinian leader Yasser Arafat denounced the UN. He said that the UN-authorised military forces sent to free Kuwait were 'not to enforce compliance with UN resolutions but to destroy Palestine . . . and make way for a greater Israel stretching from the Nile to the Euphrates'. Since then, US president George W. Bush, has recognised and called for the creation of a Palestinian state – something none of his predecessors had done. Israel has quit Gaza, the land occupied after 1967. Israel has built a wall or fence that while contested shows that claims of Israeli ambitions to push its state frontiers as far as the River Jordan, let alone the Nile or Euphrates, are not grounded in reality. In this context it is also worth recalling that Israel returned Sinai, the huge area conquered in 1967, to Egypt. It got peace with Egypt in exchange for land. It got no relief from the antisemitism that pullulates in Cairo generated by the anti-Jewish Muslim Brotherhood or from the mouths of government ministers and state-sanctioned media.

Settlement of the conflict and the dispute about Palestine and Jerusalem requires historic and heroic political leadership that neither Israelis nor Palestinians or the wider Arab community have been able to offer. There is the flattering but self-deluding notion that Washington can click its fingers and Israel comes to heel. The two stupidities on offer in America are the neo-conservative delusion that war brings democracy in its wake and, even worse, the left-liberal delusion that Washington can dictate terms to Israel or make Israeli Jews do what the US wants. A third misconception is that the European Union has the will or the vision to impose peace on a region that Europe's imperialisms turned into a chain of states that, if not failed, have never quite succeeded. The former Israeli foreign minister Shlomo Ben-Ami has described the failure of some earlier political leaders in his own country in terms of Israel's stubborn wish 'to turn down diplomatic initiatives for a settlement that did not respect the status quo created by military gains'.

As a Foreign Office minister I could not understand the

refusal of so many Arab states to have diplomatic relations with Israel. At an EU Middle East meeting, I urged Arab foreign ministers to take that simple step but I met with blank looks on the faces of men whose entire formation was based on a denial of the right of Israel to exist. Even when Germany occupied the eastern French departments of Alsace and Lorraine after the 1870 war, Paris did not break off diplomatic relations with Berlin. States may oppose each other politically, but governments are foolish when they refuse to recognise the reality of a state's existence. Britain refused to recognise Israel until 1950, as the post-war Labour government felt insulted at the manner of Israel's creation by the United Nations. Today, America remains foolish in refusing to recognise Iran. Jaw-jaw, to use Churchill's phrase, is not a replacement for war-war, but lack of jaw-jaw opens the doors more widely to those who think violence, whether by suicide bombers, military bulldozers or developing nuclear weapons, is the best means to bring about policy goals.

Both Israelis and Palestinians have missed opportunities to create opportunities. Like Lloyd George claiming he had 'murder by the throat' when he refused to countenance talking to de Valera's IRA terrorists in the Irish struggle for statehood after 1918 (and then sitting down to cut a deal), the continued refusal of Israel to talk to its Palestinian opponents unless they agreed to Israeli preconditions in the decades since 1948 has led to violence replacing diplomacy. The veteran Israeli state servant and former head of Mossad, Efraim Halevy, has written of the need to engage with both Hamas and Hezbollah, though he qualifies his position that these are 'not ideal options' and neither the Iran-sponsored Lebanese Shi'ite group, nor the Muslim Brotherhood-inspired Sunni Hamas are 'near-perfect potential partners'. Halevy, whose voice should be listened to, adds laconically, 'There is never an ideal situation and no partners are ever perfect matches.'

Thus it is hard for me as a non-Jew, as someone who can understand both the anguish of the Palestinians and the fears of Jews in Israel, to be wiser than the two Israeli policy-makers I have quoted above. If they believe that a settlement requires talking and negotiating with those who deny your right to exist on your terms – and this applies to both sides of the conflict – then who am I, sitting in the relative safety of London, to argue differently?

Maajid Nawaz is a third-generation British Muslim whose family originally came from Pakistan. He grew up in a middle-class family in Essex. At London University's presti-gious School of Oriental and African Studies (SOAS) Nawaz became a leader of the Islamist group Hizb ut-Tahrir, which he says calls for 'killing millions of people' in order to create a unified state for Muslims to live in. Nawaz served on the ex-ecutive committee of Hizb and sought to promote the Islam-ist organisation in Pakistan and Egypt. Today he has left the world of Islamist violent politics and says he 'has to make amends. What I did was damaging to British society and to the world at large.' He remains a Muslim. 'I haven't lost my religion. I've lost my ideology,' he explains.

In the House of Commons inquiry into antisemitism we heard witnesses and read material that left us shocked and depressed. Language was used about Jews that had no place in 'civilised' Britain. Writing was initiating new generations into Jew-hatred. Our tabloid papers specialise in intolerance. Contempt and dislike of eastern Europeans, especially Cath-olic Poles, asylum seekers and economic migrants, and ignor-ance of Islam as a faith are the common currency of much of our right-wing press. They are matched by crude expressions of what the writer Ian Buruma calls 'anti-Occidentalism', the dislike of the United States and of Western open democracy values in much of our left and liberal press. When Noam Chomsky wrote that in America 'what is needed is some kind of denazification' of American politics, he expressed perfectly the anti-Occidentalism Buruma defined.

As our commission carried out its work and in a classic parliamentary manner tried to make specific ameliorative policy recommendations, it was clear that something bigger was being uncovered. Antisemitism is not just about Jews today or the existence of the state of Israel. It is a new and growing ideology that as with communism or fascism seeks to replace democracy with non-democracy. Today's anti-semitism comes in many varities. It has its apologists and fellow-travellers. Lenin called the American and west Euro-pean supporters of his tyranny 'useful idiots'. Antisemitism has plenty of useful idiots, the comrades of the comrades, in place in the West's intellectual and opinion-forming classes. Christopher Hitchens is right when he links religious funda-mentalism to totalitarianism. 'In her magisterial examination of the totalitarian phenomenon,' writes Hitchens, 'Hannah Arendt was not merely being a tribalist when she gave a special place to antisemitism. The idea that a group of people – whether defined as a nation or as a religion – could be condemned for all time and without the possibility of an appeal was (and is) essentially a totalitarian one . . . But the virus was kept alive for centuries by religion.' Thus the struggle against antisemitism is also the struggle against totalitarianism. It is simultaneously a struggle to defend the Averroës-Galileo-Voltaire-Darwin values of rationalist science, free expression and Aristotelian logic.

To be sure, there are many examples of interfaith dialogue. Each community can find in the Koran, or in the examples of cooperation between Jews and Muslims, language or acts that prove the possibility of peaceful coexistence between the two religions. But the inescapable fact is that across much wider areas of the world than those where Israeli Jews and Palestinian Muslims live there is evidence of antisemitism changing the way people think, shaping how people act and winning conscious or unconscious support from a much greater number of people than ever before.

So a parliamentary inquiry into the specific fears and worries of some Jews in Britain has led into deeper waters and to the conclusion that antisemitism is a defining ideology of the twenty-first century. It is international; it is disseminated across languages and cultures; it is supported by states. Antisemitism is the political programme of clever men who have a clear and specific goal. To defeat it we need to develop an anti-antisemitism. Anti-antisemitism should be understood literally. All Semites, Arabs as much as Israelis, Muslims as well as Jews, should be protected from racism and intolerance. That means opposing those Jewish fundamentalist activists who think any criticism of Israel's occupation policies is antisemitic and whose zeal can at times come close to the censorship and intimidation they denounce in their opponents. But there is a huge difference. Unlike jihadi fundamentalists proclaiming death sentences against Salman Rushdie or Danish cartoonists, the zealots who attack critics of Israel do so within a framework of law and politics that rejects violence. A New York professor who is denied a chance of hiring a hall to criticise Israel can find hundreds of other locations to make his point. The US media, far from being controlled by the elders of an Israel lobby, cannot stop publishing books denouncing Israel and the machinations of its friends. Noam Chomsky was voted the most important intellectual in the world by readers of *Prospect*, Britain's main intellectual monthly, in 2005. Was that on account of his writings on linguistics? Or because of his lifelong animosity to Israel and his defence of Europe's most notorious anti-semite, Roger Faurisson, who wrote that 'the alleged Hitlerite gas chambers and the alleged genocide of the Jews form one and the same historical lie'?

Yet I doubt if the fixed view about Jewish power and influence that is as virulent today as it was in previous decades can be easily altered. It matters little whether US foreign policy is in the hands of realists whose relationship with Saudi money is a matter of record or the Utopian reshapers of the world who believed that removing a tyrant in Iraq would do away with tyranny. For the believer in the power of the Jews it matters little if politicians dine with antisemitic tyrants or seek to depose them. The Jew and the lobby are behind everything. As the antisemitic T. S. Eliot put it in his 1920 poem 'Burbank with a Baedeker. Bleistein with a Cigar':

> The rats are underneath the piles.
> The Jew is underneath the lot.

But that was poetry and written under very different conditions, those for whom antisemitism is an imagined problem will argue. Antisemitism, old or new, supported by states or indulged in over dinner parties, deliberate or unconscious, whether it comes from the right, the left or Islamist ideologues, remains a persistent contemporary problem and distorts political understanding of the great issue of bringing peace to the Middle East.

I

Antisemitic Parliamentarians

In his diary entry of 31 March 1982, the Conservative politician Alan Clark wrote:

> Today I asked an offensive question about Jews. It is always thought to be rude to refer to 'Jews', isn't it? I remember that slightly triste occasion, watched from the gallery, of my father being inaugurated into the Lords and my rage at Sidney Bernstein, who was being ennobled on the same afternoon and would not take the Christian oath. As loudly as I could I muttered and mumbled about 'Jews' in order to discomfit his relations who were also clustered in the gallery.
>
> I had hung it around the Foreign Secretary's visit to Israel . . . The House took it quite well, a few guffaws. It is always fun to see how far you can go with taboo subjects and titillate the House without actually shocking it.

The Cabinet Margaret Thatcher formed at the time of Clark's Old Etonian, closet Jew-baiting had Jews in it and Mrs Thatcher's own Finchley constituency had the largest share of Jewish voters of any seat in the Commons. But that did not lead to any reworking of the traditional vocabulary of sneers, jokes and barely disguised put-downs aimed at identifying Jewish Cabinet members, the most notorious being Harold Macmillan's line that the Thatcher Cabinet 'was more old Estonian than old Etonian' — a crack that sped through the bars of the Commons and in Tory clubland as a none-too-subtle way of putting Nigel Lawson, Leon Brittan or Michael Howard in their place. Over dinner in Hong Kong in the 1990s with the last governor — the liberal, whiggish, tolerant Chris Patten — I remarked that Mrs Thatcher had done well to show a British Cabinet could contain able Jewish politicians at a time when Labour was gripped by a one-sided politics on Middle East affairs. 'I don't know, Denis,' he replied. 'You should have been at the bar of the House during the Westland affair' — a reference to 1985/6 when the Jewish Cabinet member Leon Brittan was involved in a scandal over whether Britain should look to Europe or the United States for military procurement. Indeed, Sir John Stokes, a Tory MP, rose to complain that 'there are not enough red-blooded, red-faced Englishmen in the Cabinet', as dinosaur Tory antisemitism surfaced in the row over who should be installed in Brittan's place.

Pre-1939 British politics was marked by antisemitism. Some of it was notorious, like Oswald Mosley telling East Enders in 1937 council elections, 'The Jews already in this country must be sent to where they belong . . . No more admitting of foreigners into this country to take British jobs.' The dislike of the foreign worker — Jews in the 1930s for Oswald Mosley, Asians in the 1960s for Enoch Powell, Poles since 2004 for Migration Watch — is a pathology right-wing British politics can never free itself from.

And not just the right. Labour's Hugh Dalton, one of the key figures in Labour in the first half of the last century, stood for Parliament in Cardiff in 1923 against the Jewish Liberal MP Sir Alfred Mond, who founded the great chemical company that became ICI. Mond was accused of profiteering from contracts in the First World War. In a speech, Dalton won applause by referring to Mond as having never got 'beyond the Old Testament' – an obvious antisemitic jibe. John Beckett, who started as an angry left-wing Labour MP and who finished in the British Union of Fascists, is linked to Dalton by his son, Francis, who wrote his father's biography. 'There may have been a part of both John [Beckett] and Hugh Dalton which saw a connection between the fact that Mond was corrupt and the fact that he was a Jew.'

In the 1930s, the Conservative Home Secretary refused to meet a delegation from organisations combating antisemitism. Austen Chamberlain wrote of Disraeli that although he was an 'English patriot [Disraeli] was not an Englishman'. In August 1945, writing of the Conservatives, the *Jewish Chronicle* reported that 'antisemitism on the part of party supporters had led many local political associations not to select Jewish candidates'. Indeed, the first-ever Jewish Conservative MP was not elected until 1955 and until the 1970 election there were only two Jewish Tory MPs. Today's House of Commons has twenty-two Jewish MPs, of whom eleven are Conservative, eight Labour and three Liberal Democrat.

My overall impression in fifteen years as an MP is that more MPs are broadly sympathetic to the cause of Palestinians than are willing to support Israel. The former MP, now a peer, Greville Janner recalls that when he supported the Israeli attack on Iraq's nuclear arms facility in 1981, his Labour colleague Andrew Faulds turned and said, 'Go back to Tel Aviv.' Once, when Janner was in the Chamber, a colleague said, 'Your ambassador's sitting in the gallery.' It was the Israeli ambassador, and the sense that Jewish MPs are not quite British pervades. During the 1973 attack by Egypt on Israel, the Labour MP Gerald Kaufman was critical of the arms delivery embargo the Conservative government imposed on Israel. 'The Foreign Secretary, Alec Douglas Home, told me my loyalty appeared to be to Israel and not to Britain. It was a clear anti-Jewish insinuation,' recalls Kaufman, who is one of Parliament's sternest critics of Israeli policy in the occupied territories.

There are a number of MPs in All-Party Groups linked to Arab states opposed to Israel. Pro-Palestinian MPs in private conversation are venomous about Israel without ever acknowledging that from 1948 onwards, if not earlier, Palestinians could have had a state that today might be flourishing, were it not for the quality of their leaders and the policies of Arab states. Yet somehow, MPs overtly hostile to Israel, apologists for Palestinian or Arab positions and even those who make a living from business or other financial connections to Arab countries never have their Britishness called into question. Nor do they suffer the antisemitic canard of dual loyalty. When Greville Janner introduced as a peer the Archbishop of Canterbury, George Carey, two Conservative peers were overheard saying to each other: 'Who's that, introducing the Archbishop?' 'Oh, just some Jew.'

If the right has the BNP on its extreme flank, the left has Trotskyist groups. The leader of the Workers' Revolutionary Party, Gerry Healey, was denounced as 'a blatant anti-Semite' by his comrades. In the 1980s, many on the hard left in Britain used language which the late Jewish Labour MP Reg Freeson considered antisemitic. Freeson was a founding editor of the anti-fascist journal *Searchlight*. This made him a target for antisemitic attacks in the 1960s. A pig's head was nailed to his front door and a racist poster was produced with its words formed from slices of bacon. After his election to the Commons in 1964, Freeson hoped his new status would protect him, but his new opponents reverted to old hates. He described how in the 1980s he found himself routinely described in left-wing papers as 'the Zionist MP Reg Freeson'. He added, 'This term, "Zionist" was used even when the article had nothing to do with Israel, or Zionism. It was, in my view, the equivalent of the Blackshirts calling someone a "Jew-boy" in the 1930s. I went to one Labour Party meeting, where a member, a left-winger, turned to me and said: "You're a Jew, aren't you?" '

The Labour MP Oona King, whose father was an African-American political refugee witch-hunted out of the United States by McCarthyites in the 1950s, was attacked as a Jew when she defended her east London seat against the Respect Party in 2005. King's mother is Jewish. Her daughter is non-observant (though proud of her Jewish blood) and her parliamentary work focused on highlighting the Rwandan genocide and other third-world issues. But the fact her mother was Jewish gave her opponents their opening. She faced taunts like 'Get out of here, Jewish bitch' and her political opponents sought to defame her by spreading rumours that she was secretly funded by Mossad and that she wanted to ban halal meat. 'They point out I'm Jewish, and there's a Jewish world conspiracy and I must be part of it,' she wrote in her diary. 'Time and again during the general election campaign my Jewish background was used as a stick to beat me with.' Although careful to make clear that antisemitism was not the deciding factor in losing her seat, she argues that 'antisemitism was simply another factor that was skilfully manipulated for political ends'. When a Conservative candidate won a seat in 1964 campaigning under the racist slogan, 'If you want a nigger neighbour, vote Labour', he was described by Prime Minister Harold Wilson as a 'parliamentary leper', and soon lost the seat. The man who beat Oona King had already formed his own one-man parliamentary party. So there was no one to rebuke the anti-Jewish language used by some of his supporters.

In 2008, the Mayor of London, Ken Livingstone, lost his post to the anti-European right-wing Conservative, Boris Johnson. The Tory MP had used the offensive word 'piccaninnies' to describe young African children. He referred to their 'water-melon smiles'. The last MP to use the word 'piccaninnies' in British politics was Enoch Powell, who used the expression in his notorious Rivers of Blood speech which led to his dismissal from the Conservative front bench. Johnson is a serial-apologist for the offence his language has caused over the years. By contrast, his defeated opponent refused to apologise after he compared the Jewish journalist Oliver Finegold to a Nazi. Early in 2005, Finegold was reporting for the London *Evening Standard* and tried to get some quotes from Livingstone. He had a recorder with him and caught Livingstone's responses on tape as the reporter tried to put his questions to him:

LIVINGSTONE: What did you do before? Were you a German war criminal?

FINEGOLD: No, I'm Jewish. I wasn't a German war criminal . . .

LIVINGSTONE: Ah right.

FINEGOLD: I'm actually quite offended by that. So how did tonight go?

LIVINGSTONE: Well, you might be, but actually you are just like a concentration camp guard.

Unfortunately for the Mayor of London, this comparison of a Jewish journalist with a Nazi became a massive political story which resulted in considerable damage to Livingstone. He adamantly refused to apologise to Finegold. To be sure, the journalist was employed by Lord Rothermere and the Rothermere newspapers in the 1930s were notoriously anti-semitic and pro-Nazi. But Jews everywhere in Britain were shocked and hurt by the crudity of Livingstone's comparison. When the Italian Prime Minister, Silvio Berlusconi, compared a German MEP to a concentration camp guard the row exploded into an international incident with the then German Chancellor, Gerhard Schröder, cancelling his planned summer vaction in Italy to protest the Italian conservative's offensive language. In London, everyone from the Prime Minister, Tony Blair, to the Jewish deputy Mayor of London, Nicky Gavron, pleaded with Livingstone to say sorry for the offence caused. He refused. The *Guardian* journalist Jonathan Freedland wrote that Livingstone was:

> playing a dangerous game . . . Plenty of Jews cannot believe that if the mayor were confronted by, say, a black or a Muslim or gay reporter who said they were similarly hurt, he would not have made amends immediately. This is a man who prides himself on his sensitivity to London's minorities – and yet, on that night outside City Hall, he trampled on a very raw Jewish nerve, for which he has never straightforwardly apologised.

Livingstone is emblematic of many of the 1968 generation of leftist politicians for whom anti-Zionist and anti-Israel language is second nature. As editor of the *Labour Herald*, Livingstone published a cartoon in 1982 of the Israeli prime minister, Menachem Begin, dressed in black SS uniform standing on a mountain of Arab skulls above the slogan: 'The Final Solution? Shalom?' Livingstone also accused the representative body of British Jews, the Board of Deputies, of being dominated by 'neo-fascists' and argued that those Jews who supported Labour did so not 'because they were Jewish but because the Conservative Party was antisemitic'. Yet Reg Freeson, the Labour MP who was ousted and replaced as MP by Livingstone, said he did not consider the ex-London Mayor to be 'antisemitic' and as London's Mayor Livingstone supported Jewish festivals and was never short of Jews amongst his supporters. As elsewhere, the problem is one of spectrum and discourse. Where does legitimate criticism of Israel or opposition to the political ideology of Zionism end and dislike of Jews begin? When does language move from political robustness to offensive insults and then through to antisemitic discourse? Is it up to the victim to define his sense of insult and outrage? Or can the person using the language beat his chest and protest others are being too sensitive? A test might be the willingness to aplogise and to realise that offence has been caused. Boris Johnson has been willing to say sorry. Ken Livingstone was not. One of them is now Mayor of London.

In 2007, the training ground for future British political leaders, the Oxford Union, decided to invite Holocaust denier David Irving and Jew-baiting leader of the British National Party Nick Griffin to speak in a debate. The Oxford Union president was a leader of young Conservatives in Halifax in West Yorkshire where the BNP had made extensive efforts, with some success, to secure election as councillors. The BNP is rooted in antisemitism, even if today it prefers to focus on racist politics aimed at white working-class fear of the presence of black and Asian citizens.

I first saw Britain's neo-Nazis close up when the forerunner of the BNP, the National Front, organised marches in the West Midlands in support of Enoch Powell, and demanded cuts in immigration on the grounds that Britain was an 'over-crowded island' and that immigrants had access, like other citizens, to welfare benefits. As a journalist-cum-political activist in the Labour Party, I listened to the speeches of John Tyndall, leader of the National Front. Like many others, he believed in the secret power of the Jews. 'Bit by bit, it started to come home to me, in the form of incontrovertible evidence, that there was present in Britain and around the world a definite Jewish network wielding immense influence and power – through money, through politics and through its strong foothold, in some sectors amounting to virtual monopoly, in the mass media.' In his racist campaigns of the 1970s in which I heard and saw Tyndall point at lamp-posts as places to string up leaders of the 'race relations industry', antisemitism played little role. But in an article addressed to his successor, Nick Griffin, in 2004, shortly before his death, Tyndall returned to his old obsession:

> We should recognise that organised Jewry constitutes a formidable power in the world with an agenda of its own . . . we should not make a taboo of the issue of Zionism and organised Zionist power. Within party circles and in our publications we should permit a frank and free discussion of this power . . . The BNP should, so long as it is legally permissible, exclude Jews from membership.

Reading this nonsense one is tempted to dismiss it out of hand. Except that the flame of antisemitism is integral to hard right-wing politics in Britain. Nick Griffin is the fluent, Cambridge-educated leader of the BNP. With his middle-England, middle-class accent and a surface reasonableness, Griffin is popular with the editors of BBC current affairs programmes like *Today* who want to spice up their political coverage.

Griffin's main contribution to UK political debate, other than standard language on numbers of immigrants, also readily available from other right-wing sources like Migration Watch, is a desire to see Britain pull out of European Union, a political position shared by some Conservative MPs as well as outfits like the UK Independence Party (UKIP). But his main thrust is a warning about the strength of the Jewish 'lobby', which he says controls Britain's media. In one of his rare forays into consecutive writing, Griffin's long pamphlet *Who are the Mindbenders*? lists Jews who work in the media. He is particularly exercised by those, like the former BBC chairman and ITV boss Michael Grade, who do not carry the name of their immigrant ancestors. According to Griffin, 'Very few people in Britain are aware of the huge influence over the mass media exercised by a certain ethnic minority, namely the Jews.' Griffin goes on to accuse Jews of 'providing us with an endless diet of pro-multiracial, pro-homosexual, anti-British trash'. This obsession with gays seems to unite white British and Asian Muslim antisemites, though of course Griffin hates the tag antisemite. 'The mass media in Britain today have managed to implant into many people's mind the idea that it is "antisemitic" even to acknowledge that members of the Jewish community play a large part in controlling our news,' he writes. Griffin makes a selection between 'those Jews who are loyal to Britain [and] those Jews who are disloyal [to Britain], break the law and/or play a part in poisoning the public mind'.

Griffin denounced his own MP, Alex Carlisle, a Liberal-Democrat, as: 'This bloody Jew . . . whose only claim to fame is that two of his parents died in the Holocaust.' And in the Griffin right-wing world view the Jews only have themselves to blame: 'Some "antisemitism" may be provoked by the actions of certain Jews themselves and thereby have a rational basis.' Despite these efforts at ratiocination the BNP's antisemitism bubbles up like a noxious sewer overflowing into the gutter. Griffin knows that while some voters and some of the public are receptive to the BNP's anti-Asian, anti-EU, anti-Muslim message there is little tolerance for open antisemitism. Yet senior BNP councillors and BNP activists go to listen to Lady Michele Renouf, a confidante and backer of the Holocaust-denying David Irving who remains obsessed with Jews. Renouf was one of the British speakers at the antisemitic Tehran conference convened by the Iranian president Ahmadinejad in December 2006. Her speech lasted twenty minutes and was headed 'Psychology of Holocaustianity', whatever that means. It was the usual denial language, but the main political point was her call for 'a peaceful dismantling of the Israeli entity in Palestine'. Use of the word 'entity' to describe the UN-recognised state of Israel is a keyword in antisemitic vocabulary. Renouf is now a member of the so-called 'Holocaust Research Committee: Interim Committee' set up by Tehran to sustain the momentum of Iran's state-sanctioned global antisemitic politics. Its general secretary is the German-educated Dr Mohammad-Ali Ramin. He is 'a presidential adviser' to Iran's President Ahmadinejad. Ramin says that Jews 'are filthy' and has also called for the 'relocation of Israel'. Another starred international speaker alongside Lady Renouf was David Duke, the leader of America's far-right, former chief of the Ku Klux Klan and another obsessive Jew-hater. En route to Tehran, Duke spoke at a conference in Belgium with Nick Griffin.

The BNP leader's hatred of Jews has deep roots. In 1988, he published *The Rune*, which focused on Holocaust denial but added a weird twist.

Back in the 1960s the Jews quietly shifted the alleged sites of the mass gassings from the no-longer believable German camps such as Dachau and Belsen to the sites in Communist Poland such as Auschwitz and Treblinka. Now that the very idea of Zyklon-B extermination has been exposed as unscientific nonsense, they are once and again re-writing bogus history, playing down gas chambers and talking instead of 'hundreds of hitherto unknown sites in the East where more than a million Jews were exterminated by shooting'.

Dachau and Belsen were concentration camps where tortures and killings took place. Trade unionists, Social Democrats, Communists and other anti-Nazis were imprisoned along with Jews. The extermination camps the Nazis established on Polish soil organised the gassing of Jews and Roma on an industrial scale. But from the moment of the arrival of the German Army in east Europe after 1939, followed by the invasion of Hitler's erstwhile ally, Russia, in 1941, the mass shooting of Jews continued apace. Only an antisemite with Griffin's mind would see a contradiction.

More contradictions surface as we enter the tortuous ideological workings of political antisemitism. Other than Jews and Muslims, the BNP's third great hate, shared by many on Britain's far right, is the European Union and Britain's membership of the EU. Yet it is at the European Parliament – in theory the democratic home to the elected political expression of Europe's ideals – that the strongest, formal, organised political expression of antisemitism can be found. Thanks to the proportional representation electoral system, which allows a small number of votes to win parliamentary representation for extreme, sectarian or identity-based politics, twenty Members of the European Parliament now represent far-right, antisemitic political groups in the twenty-seven member states of the EU.

When initially set up, the Identity, Tradition and Sovereignty (ITS) group in the European Parliament was much smaller, of course, than the traditional party groups consisting of the centre-left Socialists, the centre-right European People's Party or the Liberals. Parties represented in the European Parliament include France's antisemitic National Front, as well as the Greater Romania Party and Bulgaria's Ataka Party, both of which are openly antisemitic. Bulgarian MEP Dimitar Stoyanov argues that: 'There are a lot of powerful Jews, with a lot of money, who are paying the media to form the social awareness of people . . . [The Jews] are also playing with economic crises in Bulgaria and getting rich.' One British MEP, Ashley Mote, became a member of the ITS group. In 2004, the BNP fell short of winning a seat in the European Parliament by a few thousand votes as the rise of the virulently anti-EU UKIP scooped up the votes of those who believe in the lies about the EU disseminated by the Europhobic tabloid press and some mainstream politicians. The leader of the ITS group was named as Bruno Gollnisch, the Lyon-based intellectual who vies with Jean-Marie Le Pen as the dominant figure in France's extreme right and antisemitic politics. Gollnisch has been condemned by French courts as a Holocaust denier. Another ITS MEP was Alessandra Mussolini, the Duce's granddaughter.

The most notorious of the European Parliament's antisemites, however, was not in the ITS group. Maciej Giertych is a Polish MEP representing the League of Polish Families. In February 2007 he published a booklet called *Civilisation at War in Europe*. The booklet was launched in Strasbourg complete with the European Parliament's logo. The Polish MEP argued that Jews are unethical, want to live obsessed with separateness and are a 'tragic community' because they don't accept Jesus as the Messiah.

It is a civilization of programmed separateness, of programmed differentiation from the surrounding communities . . . By their own will, they prefer to live a separate life, in apartheid from the surrounding communities. They form their own communes (kahals), they govern themselves by their own rule and they take care to maintain also a spatial separateness. They form the ghettos themselves, as districts in which they live together, comparable to the Chinatowns in the USA.

Giertych's son, Roman, was Poland's deputy prime minister and education minister in the right-wing government of Jaroslav Kaczynski, which lost power in September 2007. Like Islamist antisemites, Roman Giertych is hostile to gays and the teaching of evolution. The 32-page booklet by his father asserts that European culture, education and morality stem exclusively from one Christian civilisation. Poland and other Catholic nations of Europe cannot coexist in the Giertych world view with what he calls the Jews' Torah-based civilisation. When challenged, Giertych resorted to the traditional antisemitic defence that he was merely reflecting views held by others, including the ideas of the Polish historian and philosopher Feliks Koneczny, a 1930s-era philosopher who argued that Jews and Catholics could not live in the same country because Jews were lawless and immoral.

As ever, when today's antisemitic national and European parliamentarians raise their heads they are dismissed as irrelevant fringe politicians. Zygmunt Wrzodak, a Polish MP, told listeners to Poland's Radio Maryja in 2002: 'It is known that the European Union is controlled by freemasonry . . . and the interest is the following: to empower both those nations, a global Jewish nation and a European German nation.' Yet despite their antisemitic utterances these politicians are elected. Their parties, as in the case of Giertych or the Austrian elected as secretary of the ITS group, have been in government coalitions. They travel and network in Europe and link up with more extreme antisemitic Islamist politics in the Middle East. More than six decades after the defeat of Hitler, there is a worrying number of politicians in democratic Europe who embrace aspects of his antisemitic ideology. In Poland during a presidential campaign I saw posters of the then president Alexandr Kwaśniewski spray-painted with the term 'Zhid' (Yid) in order to denigrate him. The rise of nationalist anti-semitic politics can be seen in Lithuania. Jews who escaped to join the anti-Nazi partisans in Lithuania in the Second World War are now being accused by Lithuanian antisemites of taking part in war crimes. 95 per cent of Lithuania's 200,000 Jews who lived in the country before the Russian occupation in 1939 and the Nazi invasion in 1941 were killed by Germans and their Lithuanian collaborators. Lithuanian Jews who survived the Holocaust are now in their eighties, but such is the antisemitism coming back to life in some quarters of nationalist politics in the Baltic state, it has been possible to open investigations that put Jews on the same level as their executioners.

Predictably, the ITS group as a formal, fully-funded bloc in the European Parliament did not last. Mussolini's daughter attacked Romania and Romanians after a gruesome murder of an Italian woman near Rome by a Romanian. Her violent diatribes provoked fury amongst the ultra-nationalistic Romanian MEPs, who withdrew from the ITS group. Socialists and centre-right MEPs exulted in the swift disintegration of the extremist ITS group. However, they should hold their breath: the real question is why MEPs, in the name of European democracy and the EU Charter of Fundamental Rights that denounces racism and antisemitism, are so unable to take any action to stop the European Parliament from being a home to antisemitic political forces.

2

Neo-antisemitism in Europe and the World

Germany

'Germans did not invent antisemitism but Auschwitz is a German invention, which is why antisemitism in Germany is different from antisemitism anywhere else,' declared Ignatz Bubis, a leader of Germany's Jewish community. Germany takes antisemitism very seriously. It is the only European nation where there has been significant Jewish immigration in recent years – from Russia, where communities that decades or longer ago originated from Germany are allowed under German law to come back to their original Heimat. Amongst these are an important number of Jews, and the German government has financed the building of synagogues and a rabbinical school in a conscious effort to rebuild, albeit modestly, the Jewish presence in German cities prior to Hitlerism. The German government supports Germany's Jewish community with an annual subsidy of 3 million euros. When Iran's president organised his antisemitic Holocaust denial exhibition, the response of the German Foreign Ministry was not to wriggle and equivocate about such Islamist extremism but to organise its own exhibition in the summer of 2007 under the title 'Antisemitism? Antizionism? Criticism of Israel?' Germany's deputy foreign minister, Gernot Erler, was unequivocal. 'Alas, antisemitism is not where it belongs

– as a malady of the past – but it is one of Europe's contemporary phenomena which Germany's foreign policy has to deal with,' he declared. He went on to make clear to Iran and all the Islamist Jew- and Israel-haters that:

> The right of Israel to live in peace and within secure and recognised borders is and will remain for the Federal Republic of Germany a non-negotiable cornerstone of our foreign policy. Anyone, and that includes the president of Iran, who denies the Holocaust or uses hate speech against Israel or indirectly challenges Israel's right to exist, will face Germany's opposition, protest and rejection of such language.

In 1970, Germany's great post-war leader and Europe's greatest social democrat, Willy Brandt, sent a message around the world about Germany and Jews when he knelt at the Warsaw Ghetto as a symbol of penitence for what Germans had done to Jews from all over Europe thirty years previously. It was perhaps no accident that two years later the first great Islamist antisemitic atrocity in Europe took place in Munich when the Olympic Games – the millennia-old symbol of a moment when wars are forgotten – were violated by the slaughter of Jewish athletes from Israel in 1972. Munich was Hitler's beloved city and it was Nazi Germany to which the leader of the Palestinians, the Grand Mufti Husseini, came to live after 1937. *Mein Kampf* remains on sale in many Arabic, Iranian and Turkish translations and the fascination of today's Islamists for Nazis and Hitler remains an important part of contemporary antisemitism.

Those who hope that the European Union will take an anti-Israel turn have to reckon with Germany. Once at an EU Council meeting for foreign ministers I watched as the French foreign minister, Dominique de Villepin, read out a charge sheet against Israel and demanded EU presence and action on behalf of Palestinians. His speech was printed on large cards called 'Bristols' in French. As each declamatory phrase rolled out, Villepin's opposite number, the German foreign minister, Joschka Fischer, got more irritated and bored. He waited for the cards to be used up and when Villepin finished, Fischer, who inherited much of Willy Brandt's generous and wide-ranging vision on global matters (though alas he was not allowed to use his talents to the full by the German chancellor, Gerhard Schröder, and his entourage in the Kanzleramt), made clear that Germany was not going to join an anti-Israel crusade organised by French right-wingers.

In Germany and Austria, Holocaust denial, the most egregious intellectual expression of antisemitism, is illegal. So too is wearing antisemitic insignia like swastikas. Purist defenders of absolute free speech will object that to deny the Holocaust deniers their right to express their views is limiting expression. Jew-hating political groups like Hizb ut-Tahrir are banned in Germany, while successive Conservative and Labour home secretaries in Britain have refused to take action against the antisemitic Islamist outfit. Again, purists of political freedom will argue that such bans are a denial of rights. Britain's politics of extermination, racism and the invention of concentration camps (made-in-Britain terminology used to describe the camps where the families of Boer peasants and small farmers were 'concentrated' and subject to privations in order to lessen support for the Boer campaign against the English variety of white supremacism at the beginning of the twentieth century) took place in imperial and colonial possessions rather than in Europe, and Britain has never had to confront an ideological heritage like that of Nazism.

What Germans read and heard before 1933 is what they got in the years that followed. Therefore, since 1950 Germans have not been and are not prepared to take too many risks with allowing antisemitism to resurface whether in the form of Holocaust denial or allowing Islamist antisemitism or Israel-hate to pullulate on campuses any more than other forms of racist hate are permitted in Germany. In 1977, German ideological terrorists in the Red Army Faction (RAF) kidnapped the head of the German employers' federation. He was held as a hostage and photographed holding up messages just like the Islamist kidnappers of hostages in the Middle East do today. The man was murdered when the extremists had had their fun with him. The RAF were anti-Western, anti-democratic and believed in a totalising ideology in which violence would usher in a better new world. The links between German extremists and the nascent antisemitic Islamist terror groups were not disputed.

When German planes were hijacked and forced to land in the same year, the Islamists insisted on separating Jewish from non-Jewish passengers. German commandos seized back the planes but the Islamist triage of passengers into Jews and non-Jews was a reminder of the infamous arrival ramps at Auschwitz where German Nazis selected those to go straight to die and those to be sent to work and to live a little longer. Those scenes are etched deep into the German psyche of those born after 1945, who in their different ways sought to reinvent the world in the 1960s. The 1968 generation symbolised by Joschka Fischer, who had been willing to do street battles with the police to demonstrate anger at the pro-American foreign-policy choices of Willy Brandt, came to realise that the final destination of their hate march against liberal democracy was not where they wanted to go if it meant kidnapping and killing a top manager and selecting Jews for special treatment aboard a plane hijacked to protest the existence of Israel.

So today there is continuous monitoring of antisemitism in Germany. No other country produces so many serious studies on contemporary antisemitism. In terms of physical assaults on Jews or Jewish buildings, Germany differs little from the rest of Europe. In 2006, eleven Jewish cemeteries were desecrated and there were seventy-seven reported incidents in which synagogues and Jewish memorials were attacked. Opposite the apartment of my closest German friends in Frankfurt is a small synagogue. It looks like just any other building opposite a friendly pub-type restaurant in a nondescript street where ordinary Germans live. Yet outside there is usually a police car – just in case. When I read that European antisemitism really isn't much of a problem, I think of those police mounting guard in a calm, friendly Frankfurt street. The police could be better used to deal with other crime or social problems, but thanks to antisemitism they must stand guard to show that German Jews can pray in peace and security just as German Catholics and Protestants can go to their places of prayer, which do not need a police guard day and night.

Should Germany's 100,000 Jews be worried? The answer, sadly, has to be *Ja*. In a recent study, a fifth of all German students agreed with the statement 'Jews in Germany have too much influence' and 17 per cent of all those surveyed agreed that 'Jews have odd and peculiar qualities and are not really the same as us'. The Central Council of Jews in Berlin receives daily emails, letters and faxes full of anti-Jewish hate. In the land that invented the term 'antisemitism', it remains a contemporary issue. In 2006, one of the endless sociological surveys carried out in Germany reported that half of those under 30 believed that 'Israel was staging an extermination war against Palestinians'. A third of younger Germans and nearly half of over 60-year-olds believed that

Jews are trying to extract advantages from what happened in the past (i.e. the Holocaust), a view which can be defined as an example of secondary antisemitism.

Professor Armin Pfahl-Traughber, author of a classic study of antisemitism in German history, has identified six forms of antisemitism:

1. Religious antisemitism;
2. Social antisemitism;
3. Political antisemitism;
4. Racist antisemitism;
5. Secondary antisemitism;
6. Anti-Zionist antisemitism.

All these aspects of antisemitism are intermingled and are expressed in different ways in contemporary Germany despite the efforts of the German authorities to confront and deal with antisemitism. Pfahl-Traughber goes on to detail the arguments that antisemites use. They claim that Jews have always stopped Germans from living in harmony with nature and each other, and that they invented capitalism, liberalism, socialism and feminism and spread these unhealthy ideas throughout the world. In Pfahl-Traughber's analysis, contemporary German antisemites believe Jews have been able to achieve this remarkable degree of influence because they control the media, pull government strings and control the world economy. This world conspiracy of Jews explains most modern history from the French Revolution to 9/11. Jews also stand for a merciless universalism because they accentuate the difference between the people (*Volk*) and culture. Jews themselves are responsible for antisemitism because they refuse to assimilate and integrate fully. For modern antisemites their hate of Jews and their opposition to Israel is inextricably mixed together. There is a mushy grey zone, which begins with anti-Israel utterances and drifts into anti-semitism. The exact frontier between opposition to Israel and opposition to Jews is hard to define. But Jews refuse to draw a line under the past by their insistence on Holocaust commemoration and education, argue the antisemites, according to Pfahl-Traughber.

The most organised antisemitism in Germany comes from extreme right-wing parties and their loosely linked groups of supporters, fellow-travellers or sympathisers. They belong in the same family of politics as the BNP in Britain or the National Front in France. Germany's extreme right knows that Holocaust denial is a crime under German law so the formal party structures are careful to avoid, as far as possible, overt anti-Jewish statements. One of the more prominent German antisemites, Horst Mahler, was forced to leave the extreme-right NPD (National Democratic Party) to launch his 'Association for the Rehabilitation of those Persecuted for Denying the Holocaust'. German courts have taken tough action against persistent Holocaust deniers, but always at the risk of the antisemites portraying themselves as political martyrs. Modern German antisemitism with its self-pitying focus on Jews continuing to go on and on about the Holocaust, and its claim that those sent to prison for antisemitism are 'political martyrs', thus links up with Islamist antisemitism's claims that the Holocaust is a myth and that today's martyrs are those who confront Jews and the Jewish state.

French Intellectuals and Antisemitism

Holocaust denial also lies at the heart of French antisemitism. Other than Germany and Russia in the late nineteenth century, France had been home to the most virulent antisemitic politics. This culminated in the Dreyfus affair, the moment when Theodor Herzl said he decided that without their own home or state, Jews would never be absolutely sure of their safety in Europe. Céline, France's best-selling writer of the inter-war years, was openly antisemitic. In one play he claimed the League of Nations was a Jewish conspiracy – anticipating the Hamas Charter denunciation of the United Nations as a Jewish creation. When the French Popular Front government was set up, Céline wrote, 'I would prefer a dozen Hitlers to one omnipotent Blum', a reference to the Jewish Socialist prime minister, Léon Blum, who was a particular target for French antisemites. In the Second World War, senior French officials collaborated with the Nazis to deport Jews to the extermination camps located in east Europe. Jean-Paul Sartre in 1946 wrote a short book, *Reflections on the Jewish Question*, which argued in the fashion of Voltaire that 'if the Jew did not exist, the anti-semite would have to invent him'. In other words antisemitism is an ideology of nationalist hate, which constantly paints the Jew as a target – whether the Jewish lobby, the Jewish state, the Jewish businessman, the Jewish editor. Sartre finished with these premonitory words: 'The cause of the Jews would already be half won if only their friends found in their defence a little of the passion and the perseverance that their enemies devote to their destruction . . . No Frenchman will be secure as long as a Jew, in France or elsewhere in the world, has reason to fear for his life.' Alas, Sartre's zigzagging political and philo-sophical trajectory over the rest of his life left him often supporting causes or movements that were impregnated with exactly the antisemitism he condemned.

French Communists denounced Jewish Communist politi-cians in east Europe as 'American spies' during the last show trials of the Stalin era. Again, we can read one of today's tropes emerging as the French left sought to make a distinction between anti-Zionism and antisemitism. Gilles Martinet, a pillar of the non-communist left who was named as ambassador to Italy by François Mitterrand in 1981, assured readers asking why Jews figured so large in the show trials in Prague in 1952 that 'Antizionism must not be confused with antisemitism'. Some important left intellectuals and journalists, like Claude Bourdet, did insist on the 'systematic use of antisemitic passions' by east European communist regimes, but Bourdet was rebuked in *L'Humanité*, the French Communist daily, which wrote of the 'the well-deserved punishment of Zionist criminals working for American spy agencies'. During the 1967 Middle East conflict, General de Gaulle sneered at Jews as 'an assertive and domineering people'. The General's contempt was taken up by the leftists of the 1968 generation, who wrote in 1973 in *L'Humanité rouge* that 'zionism is fascism' or, linking up with classic Islamist language, that 'it is the very existence of Israel that is the source of the Middle East conflict'. As François Furet wrote in 1978, 'In today's thinking, the conquering Israeli has taken the place of the Jewish plutocracy that the right and the left of the nineteenth century believed existed.'

De Gaulle and his successors – until the arrival in 1995 of Jacques Chirac in the Elysée – refused to accept French responsibility and culpability for the antisemitic laws passed by France after 1940. They hid behind the fiction that the Vichy government was not the government of France and therefore France as a nation did not have to say sorry about its treatment of Jews by French government officials between 1940 and 1944.

This sullen refusal to accept the consequences of antisemitism came back to life in the 1970s as French antisemitic intellectuals picked up and developed into a major political theory the concept of negationism – Holocaust denial. This had been developed as early as 1950 by Paul Rassinier, whose politics began in the French Communist Party before he joined the Socialists of Léon Blum in the 1930s. Captured in the resistance, he was deported to Buchenwald. He was briefly a French MP but lost his national assembly seat in 1946 to the Jewish socialist Pierre Dreyfus-Schmidt, a distant relative of the famous Captain Dreyfus. This seems to have triggered a retreat to a leftist antisemitism, which emerged in his book *Le Mensonge d'Ulysse* (*The Lie of Ulysses*) published in 1950. The book blamed an international Jewish lobby for unleashing the Second World War and accused Jews of inventing reports of mass killings in the gas chambers of the Nazi extermination camps in Poland. In 1964, Rassinier published a book, *Le Drame des Juifs Européens* (*The Drama of the European Jews*), which claimed that the really dramatic event was 'not that six million Jews were exterminated as they claim but rather in the fact that they make the claim'.

Negationism or Holocaust denial is one of the most important post-war expressions of antisemitism that took a strong hold in French intellectual circles and anti-Jewish political circles. Louis Darquier de Pellepoix, the Vichy minister in charge of Jews, told the French magazine *L'Express* in 1978: 'The only things gassed at Auschwitz were lice.' He was followed by France's champion Holocaust denier, Roger Faurisson, a university professor of literature, who denied the existence of gas chambers. 'The invented massacre of Jews and the invented existence of gas chambers unite to create the political-financial fraud whose main beneficiaries are the state of Israel and the international Zionist movement', Faurisson told French radio.

In the 1980s, the views of Faurisson were propagated by the French National Front party and its Jew-baiting leadership. Unlike the marginal antisemitic right-wing parties in Britain or Germany, Jean-Marie Le Pen's National Front scored up to 20 per cent of the French vote in legislative elections and beat the French Socialist candidate, Lionel Jospin, into third place in the 2002 presidential election. I attended one of Le Pen's meetings in southern Brittany in the late 1980s. He constantly invoked the names of Pierre Mendès-France and Laurent Fabius, the two Jewish centre-left prime ministers in post-war France. Le Pen did not attack them directly as Jews, but the manner in which he hissed out their names, pouring his Jew-hate into an ugly intonation as he accused them of betraying France, left his eager listeners in no doubt that these two were being singled out because they were Jewish. Outside the giant tent where Le Pen harangued his followers, activists sold posters with a hook-nosed Mendès-France and posters accusing Fabius of allowing French children to be contaminated by AIDS-infected blood. Once again, the blood libel resurfaced as French antisemitism found new life with hate of Israel and hate of Jews in public life.

Jean Marie Le Pen and his lieutenants sought to avoid overt, sustained antisemitic utterances but could not prevent themselves from referring to the Holocaust as a 'detail of history' or embracing the popular French-African comedian Dieudonné M'Bala M'Bala, who said in 2004 that Jews had been slave traders in the past and today controlled banks and the entertainment industry. Le Pen's No. 2, Bruno Gollnisch, was still facing charges of Holocaust denial in 2007, while Roger Faurisson was broadcasting into France via the Iranian satellite channel, Sahar 1, his views that the Nazis did not exterminate Jews because there were no gas chambers at Auschwitz.

Roger Garaudy was a leading French Communist after 1945

who was in the forefront of ideological attacks against Stalin's opponents. Like many he left the faith of the 'God that failed', but over the years found a new cause – that of attacking Jews. In 1998, he was condemned by a French court for writing lies about the Holocaust. But as France has rejected him, the Arab world has embraced him. Egypt's most important Muslim cleric, Grand Sheikh Mohammed Sayed Tantawi, heads the Al-Azhar mosque and as such is seen as one of the highest authorities in Sunni Islam. In February 2007, he rolled out the red carpet for a visit by Garaudy to Cairo. Sheikh Tantawi has in the past condemned suicide bombings, including those in Israel. These contingent statements can be found but do not form part of a coherent rejection of antisemitic ideology. The sheikh, in honouring Garaudy, who is considered in France to be an antisemitic politician with a left-wing past, appeared to indicate where his true sympathies lay.

This century, the French Socialist Party was tempted to seek French Muslim votes by attacking Israel in the form of a report written by one of its national secretaries, Pascal Boniface. He argued that French Jews 'underline their electoral weight to create an impunity for the Israeli government . . . but the Muslim community has more votes'. The suggestion that support for the right of Israel to exist should be sacrificed on the altar of Muslim votes caused outrage when Boniface made his argument before the 2002 elections. Far from helping the Socialist candidate, Socialist activists said the anti-Israel tenor, which can be found elsewhere in democratic centre-left parties in Europe so far this century, caused Jewish voters to reject the Socialist Party.

In 2005, a team of sociologists headed by France's foremost researcher into racism, Michel Wieviorka, investigated the depth and range of antisemitic thinking amongst Muslims in

France. In the socially deprived suburbs where French urban planners dumped the massive north African population hoovered into France to do all the dirty, low-paid, boring and dangerous jobs that white French citizens did not want to do, the extent of antisemitic feeling is depressing and disturbing. Swastikas were found on the lifts serving the tall apartment blocks where poor Muslim families live. Walls were sprayed with anti-Jewish insults and in every interview the team of researchers carried out they recorded vile anti-semitic epithets and abuse. All independent research studies show an alarming degree of anti-Jewish feeling amongst France's five million Muslims. Islamist organisations with differing links to Islamist movements abroad make a point of attacking Israel at every opportunity. Many French intellectuals and political activists on the left suspend critical judgement when it comes to the Middle East.

In January 2006, a mobile phone salesman, Ilan Halimi, a Jew, was captured by a gang led by the Jew-hating Youssof Fofana. They tortured Halimi, shouting antisemitic abuse at him as he screamed in pain. Halimi died as a result of the torture. The gang told the police that they had chosen Halimi because he worked in a Jewish-owned shop in a Jewish area of Paris. Jews were rich, they said, and therefore would pay a large ransom for the release of their co-religionist. When police raided Fofana's home they found neo-Nazi and anti-semitic material downloaded and printed from an Islamist website.

It is too easy, however, to point a finger only at those inspired to make antisemitic remarks or worse by Islamist ideology. The French intellectual Stéphane Zagdanski argues in his book *De l'antisémitisme* that, 'There is today no less antisemitism in France than during the Occupation or at any other moment in the history of France.' He cites other contemporary French writers who argue that the word 'Jew' has lost all meaning since 1945 and that Israel as a Jewish state has become an antisemitic state. Zagdanski's dense, complex argument was corrected by Théo Klein, a former head of France's Jewish community and a resistance leader in the Second World War, who argues for 'the clear distinction between feelings that may exist in a population and the political situation'. Today's France is not as antisemitic as in the time of Dreyfus or when Jews were handed over to the Nazis for deportation, but even a cursory reading of French books and intellectual writing reveals a fear that antisemitism in France is a part of twenty-first-century politics, as it was in previous centuries.

Take for example the giant French perfume company L'Oréal. It has been held up to shame in France over its handling of property stolen from a Jewish family in Karlsruhe, Germany by the Nazis. In a powerful account, *L'Oréal Took My Home*, Monica Waitzfelder describes her unending struggle with one of the world's most powerful cosmetic-industry multinationals to obtain redress and reparation for the loss of her home on account of her family's Jewishness. Denying the Holocaust and refusing responsibility for French complicity in crimes against Jews are both in their different ways reminders of France's continuing problem of anti-semitism.

Yet I know and love France, and my children have French as well as British nationality. France is not an antisemitic country, any more than Britain is. But there is now a wide spectrum of political activism in France that causes fear and concern amongst French Jews. When Dieudonné turned up to embrace Jean-Marie Le Pen and to exclaim, 'He is the real right and I am the real left,' was he aware of Le Pen's views on Jews or his statement made in January 2005 that the Nazi 'occupation of France was not particularly inhuman'? But then, when asked about Dieudonné's antisemitic references in his shows, Le Pen said he thought they were 'funny'. When Raymond Barre in March 2007 spoke of the Jewish 'lobby' in France, did he know that they were the terms used by all the most extreme Jew-hating Islamist groups around the world? When the Francophone Tariq Ramadan identifies as Jews some of France's most respected thinkers and writers as he reproaches them for not following his line on international politics, does he pause to reflect what impact making an intellectual's Jewishness a line of attack might have on the untutored mind of a Muslim youth potentially attracted to vandalism or crime?

Antisemitism is not new in France. It has waxed and waned over 150 years. On each occasion antisemites have found new justification for their hate campaigns. In the nineteenth century French antisemites blamed Jewish money for France's woes; in 1936, they accused the Jewish Léon Blum of betraying France; French Stalinist antisemites attacked Jews placed on Communist show trials in east Europe in the 1950s; a decade later French antisemitism was expressed at the highest level after Israel's defeat of Arab armies in 1967; in the 1980s, Le Pen attacked Jewish campaigns to highlight French complicity in the Holocaust; and finally, in this century, Jewish intellectuals who refuse to denounce Israel's right to exist and defend itself are attacked by Tariq Ramadan because they are Jews, not because they hold different political views from Islamists and *Le Monde Diplomatique*. Sometimes the antisemitic attacks come from the nationalist, ultra-Catholic right, sometimes from the anti-American, anti-globalisation left, and today from the Islamist political forces who are well organised and well financed in France. But whatever the excuse, the target of hate, leading in the case of Ilan Halimi to his death, remains constant.

Global Neo-antisemitism

This obsession that makes Jews the objects of envy and contempt and worse is not limited to the European continent. It is truly a global phenomenon. The hideous displays of Jew-hatred at the infamous UN Conference against Racism, Racial Discrimination, Xenophobia and Related Intolerances in Durban in August 2001 at which posters were displayed of a picture of Hitler with the words: 'What If I had Won? There would be NO Israel and No Palestinian's Blood Shed' and copies of *The Protocols of the Elders of Zion* were on sale shocked all the delegations from democratic countries present. They spurred the work by the OSCE (Organization for Security and Co-operation in Europe) and the European Union to create special committees and rapporteurs as the democratic world woke up to the extent to which Jew-hatred had re-entered the international community, with the backing of some states and the tolerance of too many others. I was a newly appointed minister in the British government at this period and busy travelling in Latin America. The full extent of the antisemitic orgy taking place at the Durban conference, especially in the NGO parallel sessions, was not fully appreciated until after the event. I hope had I represented Britain at that event I would have had the courage to pull out the UK delegation and risk the wrath of superiors in Whitehall who were bending over backwards to placate Islamist ideologues, including those who have supported the murder of innocent Jewish children and women. As I read with mounting concern the raging hate against the Jewish people expressed at the conference and its linked events, the scales began to fall off my eyes about the way the democratic governments of the world had underestimated the arrival of latter-day antisemitism as a new organising force in world politics.

Ever tempted by antisemitism are those countries where populist and nationalist forces are given free reign. When the politics of economics fails to deliver equitable growth, material satisfaction and a degree of social justice, the politics of identity take over. Latin American populists like Juan Perón in Argentina, or his contemporary successor Hugo Chávez in Venezuela, have been tempted by antisemitism. Argentina has a large population of Jews, about 1 per cent of the population, the same as in France. Perón opened Argentina's borders after 1945 to Nazis fleeing from efforts in post-war Europe to bring to justice those responsible for the ultimate expression of antisemitism, the mass killings of Jews. Adolf Eichmann should have been put on trial and hanged in Europe, not helped to escape to Latin America until his capture by Israeli agents and subsequent rendition to stand trial in Israel. Despite the large number of Jews in Argentina, top state positions in the foreign or military service were closed to Argentinian Jews. When the military junta seized power in 1976, under the benevolent eye of Washington, the number of Jews arrested, detained and tortured was out of all proportion to the non-Jewish citizens of Argentina. Ten times as many Jews as non-Jews were arrested when the junta took over government. The famous Argentinian journalist and writer Jacobo Timerman, in his book *Prisoner Without a Name, Cell Without a Number*, recalls how his interrogators kept asking him about the 'worldwide Jewish conspiracy'. Other Jewish victims of the military round-up reported that their torturers would shout Nazi-linked insults at them as they tried to extract information about Jewish organisations and personalities.

In 1971, five years before the *golpe*, a nationalist politician called Walter Beveraggi Allende revealed what he called 'Plan Andinia', which he said was a 'Zionist project' to create a new Jewish state in Patagonia. In 1976, the year of the military takeover, Allende published a book *From the Zionist Yoke to the Possible Argentina*, which repeated the Plan Andinia nonsense and added extra antisemitic encouragement to the Argentinian rightists who backed the overthrow of democracy. The military junta permitted the publication of antisemitic journals. One, *Occidente* (West), had a big swastika on the cover of its first issue. This latter-day effort to create the same hates as the authors of *The Protocols of the Elders of Zion* aimed for might be laughed away as nonsense save that thirty years later in 2003, the Army Chief of Staff made similar allegations in a lecture at the nation's staff college. General Bendini was reported to have said that the army was concerned by the 'pretensions of foreign powers over Patagonia' and among the 'suspects [were] Israelis arriving in the country ostensibly as tourists'. In the murky world of recent manoeuvring by the politicians and top generals in Argentina, the full extent of the alleged remarks was not proven. But once antisemitic conspiracy theories have entered a nation's political DNA they remain for a long time.

In 1993, antisemites planted a bomb in a Jewish community building in Buenos Aires, killing more than eighty Jews in the largest single antisemitic attack since the Nazi era. After long delays and under considerable international pressure, the Argentinian authorities issued arrest warrants and accused Iran and Hezbollah of being involved in the attack. However, those responsible for attacking the Israeli embassy in 1992 have never been found. Many in Argentina consider that a shadowy network of right-wing, Nazi-sympathising antisemites was responsible and they were still carrying out the antisemitic politics that had been given cover at the highest level of the state, military and church in Argentina ever since the 1940s. Slogans seen sprayed on Buenos Aires streets in 2006 included 'Death to the dirty Jews' and 'Commit a patriotic act: kill the Jews'. Jorge Abib, a senator in the province of Cordoba, told radio listeners during the 2006 Israel-Lebanon conflict that, 'The Jews put the bomb [in the community building in 1993]. What Hitler did to the Jews was a good thing.'

Further north, the repeated visits to Tehran and warm embrace by the Venezuelan president, Hugo Chávez, of his Iranian confrère, President Ahmadinejad, alarmed Jews in Venezuela who took seriously the antisem-itic utterances of the Iranian leader. Speaking alongside Ahmadinejad, in July 2006, Chávez said that 'a force will emerge . . . that will put an end to the empire [i.e. Israel] and its people'. In Damascus in August 2006, Chávez pleased his hosts in the capital of the Syrian dictatorship when he described the Jewish state as 'a creation of the North American empire in the Middle East' and blamed Israel as 'the reason for the conflict in the area'. Neither history nor causality could deflect Chávez as he continued his tirades, which were in complete alignment with the banal antisemitic tropes of the Jew-hating Islamist and Arab propagandists of the Middle East.

It is not only Venezuela's leader. Many media moguls in the country hate Chávez from a rabidly right-wing standpoint. This deep reactionary conservatism also foments an antisemitism from the right to match Chávez's antisemitism from the left. Most Venezuelan papers carry virulent anti-Jewish columns and articles. Venezuela, like many Latin

American countries, has a press that carries lengthy opinion-
and-comment articles and much less factual reporting based
on deontological attempts to achieve accuracy and balance.
The Lebanese conflict and the green light to attacks on Jews
and Israel by the country's president opened the way to
articles as ugly in their dislike of Jews as any published in
the Middle East. '*Los judios sionistas*' was typical of many
opinion pieces. Written anonymously and published in *El
Diario de Caracas* in September 2006, the article claimed that
the Zionists would again suffer a Holocaust because of the
world's hate for Jews who 'are without a homeland because
they killed Christ'.

The image of Jews as Christ-killers had been used the
previous year by Chávez in a speech denouncing global
capitalism when he said that the 'descendants of those who
killed Christ' had 'taken possession of all the wealth in the
world'. Hugo Chávez remains a hero for many in the world
who long for a charismatic figure willing to use his state
office to denounce the United States. I have met Chávez
in his presidential office late at night in Miraflores, the
unassuming building in the middle of Caracas which houses
the presidency. I sensed no arrogance or evil design in a
soldier disgusted with the failings of the super-rich, self-
serving elites who in Venezuela as elsewhere in Latin America barely know the poor exist. He seeks to please the
listener and talked to me positively about the example of
the European Union as a model Latin America could follow
in place of the high tariff walls and other barriers between
states that stop trade, wealth and social justice growing.
Capitalism in Venezuela is under no threat from Chávez
providing the capitalists keep to their business activities
and do not support anti-Chávez democratic politics. Venezuela's oil wealth allows Chávez to be generous. In his red

beret, he is like a male Evita distributing largesse to the poor of Venezuela, who have been ill-served by their political elites.

What is harder to explain is this stubborn embrace for some of the most loathsome Jew-haters in the world like Iran's Ahmadinejad, who was addressed by Chávez as 'My brother'. Nor why it is necessary in far-away Venezuela for Chávez to bring to the surface the populist, nationalist anti-semitism that simmers in the cauldron of South American political discourse. Chávez can fantasise that his oil-financed populism is a new twenty-first-century socialism. He can sit at Castro's bedside while writers and journalists rot in Cuban prisons. He can make common cause with other oil producers. He can denounce the United States. But why pick on Jews? Truly, antisemitism has its uses. Chávez does not need to be a Jew-hater, but antisemites venerate their new champion in Caracas. A fifth of Venezuela's Jewish population has left the country since Chávez became president in 1999. Like the canary in the coal mine, antisemitism is an indicator of worse to follow. Chávez himself denies any anti-Jewish intentions, but as the Venezuelan commentator Sammy Eppel notes: 'They're not burning synagogues or persecuting people in the streets but there is officially sanctioned antisemitism. The Venezuelan people aren't antisemitic. This is being directed by a few activists.'

Japan: Antisemitism Without Jews

Japan, which has very few Jews, still manages to produce antisemitic writings and politics. *The Protocols of the Elders of Zion* was widely translated in the 1920s after the Japanese Army confronted the new Soviet Union. In 1905 it had been the Japanese who humiliated the Russian imperial fleet. Thirty years later it was the turn of Russian tank divisions, ably led by the young General Zhukov, to defeat the Japanese Army as it sought to extend its base in Manchuria into Siberia. As Japan linked up with Nazi Germany in the Anti-Comintern Axis, the *Protocols* were translated and publicised to 'prove' that Japan faced threats from international Jewry. Yet Shanghai under Japanese occupation proved a refuge to thousands of European Jews who fled from the antisemitism of the 1930s and after the Nazi conquests of European nations in 1939 and 1940. Japanese cruelty to Asian victims of Japanese imperial militarism knew few limits, but although the European Jews in Shanghai suffered the same privations as other Europeans interned there from 1942 onwards, there were no specific anti-Jewish measures and no suggestion of the extermination politics of European antisemitism. After the war, or rather after the return of Japan as a major economic power from the 1970s onwards, Japanese nationalists, populists and leftists indulged in a revived antisemitism. A Christian propagandist, Masami Uno, wrote best-sellers in the 1980s that accused Jews of provoking trade and other disputes between the United States and Japan. There was a secret 'shadow government' of Jews in America who controlled US policy. His books sold over a million copies. The title of one published in 1986 was *If You Understand the Jews, You Will Understand the World*. He urged Japanese leaders to imitate Adolf Hitler and keep the Japanese race pure. The efforts to promote democracy in Japan since 1945 and to make Japan a country engaged as a market democracy in world affairs amounted to nothing less than the 'Judaisation of Japan'.

A respected economics professor, Yajima Kinji, published

his *Expert Way to Read the Jewish Protocols* in 1986. Within a year it had been reprinted fifty-five times! At the same time, the sect Aum Shinrikyo was founded by the bearded, half-blind Shoko Asahara, whose features and messianism bear uncanny resemblance to some of the Islamist preachers of hate who have pullulated in Britain until the sleeping mask dropped from government eyes after 7/7. By most standards the attacks of the Aum sect, which used toxic sarin gas released from a lorry in Tokyo in 1994, killing seven, and followed it up with another gas attack on the Tokyo subway the following year, which killed twelve and injured 5,000, were insane. Three months before the 1995 attack, the official organ of the sect declared 'war' on the Jewish 'shadow world government' that sought to 'murder untold numbers of people and . . . control the rest'. Japanese political publishing linked to extremist ideas and nationalist movements is a phenomenon that is peculiar to the country. A short book I wrote about the Polish union, Solidarity, was quickly translated into Japanese. It was not from any interest in Polish workers or sympathy for trade unionism but, as I later discovered, because the publisher was a leading anti-Soviet writer and propagandist and simply wanted to highlight the anti-communist nature of the Polish trade union. So the millions of copies of manic antisemitic books sold in the 1980s should be seen more in the context of Japanese nationalism and concerns that the country's Nippon identity was under threat from globalisation and Westernism, rather than Japan succumbing to Islamist or classical Western Jew-hatred and Israel-hatred. Yet the choice of gas as the weapon of attempted mass murder and the open invocation of Nazi-style exterminationist designs underlines how the history of the worst aspects of antisemitism can be brought back to life.

Japan is not antisemitic and has few Jews living there. But antisemitism does not need Jews to poison minds and unleash evil.

3

The Campus Breeding Grounds

All forms of antisemitism are bad, but some are more worrying than others. Universities should, in theory, be the last place where Jews in liberal democracies should feel ill at ease. The antisemitism of the campus is now a serious problem. It is university teachers like Roger Faurisson in France who have used their academic posts to generate the hateful denial of the Holocaust, an insult to the millions of Jews around the world who live daily with the memory of family gassed and cremated to satisfy Hitler's antisemitic desires. American universities have long given tenure and shelter to academics who are careful never to criticise Jews outright, but instead revert to old metaphors about networks of Jewish influence and, of course, relentless criticism of Israel.

It is vital for the global antisemitism movement to win the hearts and minds of the young. Give me a child until he is seven and I will give you the man, said the Jesuits, as they realised that controlling the schools of Catholic Europe would be the greatest service they could render the Church. So too, the call of the Jew-haters is to win over as many young minds as possible to hatred of Israel and to a belief that Jews constitute a malign conspiracy of control. It is on university campuses that serious money is spent to export the Jew-hating theo-ideology of Wahhabism.

Anti-Jewish political groups like Hizb ut-Tahrir seek to

have a formal presence on campuses. This is how Ed Husain, recalling his time as a college student in London, describes what he calls the 'Islamist control of the Muslim student population . . . At many universities the tactics of confrontation and consolidation of Muslim feeling under the leadership of Hizb activists were being adopted. The Hizb confronted the Jewish . . . lecturers . . . What dumbfounded us was the fact that the authorities on campuses never stopped us.' Husain had been attracted to Islamism as a schoolboy. A poster in his bedroom quoted the famous appeal of Hasan al-Banna, the grandfather of Tariq Ramadan and founder of the Muslim Brotherhood.

> Allah is our Lord.
> Mohammed is our Leader.
> The Koran is Our Constitution.
> Jihad is Our Way.
> Martyrdom is Our Desire.

All over the world students at school or university put up posters of 'revolutionary' heroes like Che or Mao, today Hugo Chávez or Sheikh Nasrallah, without thinking through what they really stand for or have done. But how many have gone to sleep having done their homework under a poster urging jihad and expressing a desire for martyrdom?

At his college, Husain helped cover the college walls as well as the street outside with posters reading 'Islam: The Final Solution' because 'deep down, we never really objected to the Holocaust . . . Without question we despised Jews and perceived a Jewish conspiraracy.' Like a con man who changes his name as he moves from town to town, Hizb is also adept at adopting new guises as it seeks to win over students to its antisemitic core beliefs. Islamist spokesmen have denounced Husain's exposé of Hizb anti-Jewish work on campuses as being a lone example of what happened in the 1990s. Yet the All-Party Parliamentary Inquiry into Anti-semitism reported that in December 2005, the Muslim Public Affairs Committee UK organised a debate under the title 'Zionism: The Greatest Enemy of the Jews'. Some of the listed speakers were known to have expressed antisemitic opinions on previous occasions and the university cancelled the event. MPACUK riposted on its website saying 'Jewish Societies' were the same as 'Zionist Societies'. It accused Jewish students of working for Mossad and put up a picture of Spider-Man using the classical anti-semitic motif of Jews spinning a web of control. In 2002, the University of Manchester Students' Union discussed a motion that anti-Zionism was not antisemitism. The General Union of Palestinian Students distributed a leaflet before the vote that repeated classic antisemitic propaganda including the Benjamin Franklin forgery circulated by the Nazis, which claimed the American statesman had written an anti-Jewish tract in the eighteenth century that called Jews 'vampires'. The motion was defeated. The response of the Jew-haters was to throw a brick through the window of a Jewish student residence and a poster with the words 'Slaughter the Jews' was stuck on the front door.

So far from Ed Husain's description of Islamist anti-semitism on the campus being an isolated example from the 1990s, the Jew-hate in British universities has intensified this century. In 2005, the Glasgow-based national Scottish paper *The Herald* reported on the efforts of Hizb, and other Islamist groups with different names, but sharing the same political gene pool and anti-Jewish obsessions as Hizb, to infiltrate Scottish universities. A Hizb spokesman admitted that the extremist organisation was seeking to work 'in Glasgow, Dundee and Edinburgh universities'. Al-Muhajiroun, the breakaway group from Hizb and arguably even more violent in its antisemitism, was also active in Dundee and other universities. According to *The Herald*, Dundee University 'said it had no knowledge of radical Islamic groups being active on its campus' while 'Edinburgh University said it . . . did not object to religious groups holding meetings on campus as long as they operated within the law and did not deploy inappropriate tactics'. But both Hizb and Al-Muhajiroun exist to snuff out free speech and replace democracy. They are not religious groups in the sense of Quakers, Buddhists, Mormons or Orthodox Christians who wish to share their views on faith with others. Hizb and its offshoots are deeply political and refuse to join in campaigns to condemn attacks on Jews worldwide.

The National Union of Students seeks valiantly to combat such hate extremism and has adopted a 'No Platform' policy that seeks to urge each NUS body on each campus to reject the efforts of the Hizb-BNP-Al-Muhajiroun alliance against Jews. The antisemitic BNP is also active on campuses seeking supporters for resolutions at students' unions that call for complete free speech. This attractive-sounding proposition is aimed at efforts of democratic students' unions to deny platforms on the campus to hate speech and those who, of course, deny all free speech in countries where their ideology wins power. A Hizb spokesman, Dr Imran Waheed, also lined up with the BNP when he said, 'We are trying to overturn the NUS ban which we believe is completely unjustified.'

Jewish students, like Muslim students or students of any kind, should feel free in their universities from the hate that may confront them in wider society. The role of the liberal university tradition is to defend liberty, not to promote politics that reduce liberty. One would have thought that all adults who teach at or administer our universities would subscribe to that vision. One might also assume that university teachers would live in some relation to reality. Now listen to these three American academics. Natana DeLong-Bas, a lecturer in theology at Boston College, as well as in the Department of Near East and Judaic Studies at Brandeis University, says that she does 'not find any evidence that makes me agree that Osama Bin Laden was behind the attack on the Twin Towers. All we have heard from him was simply praise and commendation of those who had carried out the operation.' And she is allowed to guide the minds of the young? Or Joseph Massad, a Columbia University professor of modern Arab politics and intellectual history, who has written 'all those in the Arab world who deny the Holocaust are, in my opinion, Zionists'. Sorry. Can we read that again? Holocaust deniers are Zionists? What else does this man believe? Then there is Hatem Bazian, a senior lecturer in Islamic studies at University of California, Berkeley, who states that 'it's about time that we have an intifada in this country that changes fundamentally the political dynamics in here'. Perhaps my generation of Brits who spent much of our adult lives worrying about the terrorist bombs and sectarian killings of the IRA and Unionist supremacists won't find that funny.

It is fashionable amongst American campaigners against antisemitism to paint Europe as being in the grip of a virulent Jew- and Israel-hating movement. However, it is on American campuses that some of the worst examples of antisemitic behaviour and words can be found. In October 2001, just after 9/11, students at New York University handed out copies of articles by David Duke, the leading American right-winger. Duke argued that, 'The primary reason we are suffering from terrorism in the United States is because our government policy is completely subordinated to a foreign power: Israel and the efforts of worldwide Jewish suprema-cism.' In April 2002, a student called a fellow student, a Jew, at the University of Denver a 'kike' during a demonstration against Israel. On the same day, at the University of Califor-nia, Berkeley, antisemitic students attempted to storm and break up a Holocaust Remembrance Day event. 'Fuck Jews' was sprayed at a Jewish student centre. Further up the coast, students produced posters showing soup cans saying the contents were 'Palestine Children Meat'. Students at San Francisco State University in 2002 put up posters saying 'Jews=Nazis.'

Phyllis Chesler is an American academic and one of the United States' most respected feminist authors. She spans the modern American university and intellectual left from its reincarnation as a collection of political *enragés* in the 1960s to modern times. Her book, *The New Anti-Semitism*, is a pas-sionate account of her personal engagement with fellow academics, feminists and intellectuals. Like many who have come to realise the dangers of an ideologised and state-backed antisemitism, she is critical of Israel. Chesler says Israel is a 'theocratic state, which means that the state holds individuals – women especially – captive to a sacralized miso-gyny'. She is critical of Israel's treatment of Arab citizens living within Israel's pre-1967 borders. 'Israel Arabs were not granted equal citizenship. This is unforgiveable, an under-standable but huge mistake.' She develops her criticism with passion. Yet the purpose of her book is not to argue for a different Israel, but to name and shame the antisemites she sees at work in her world of US intellectual and university life. This in some ways is the greatest victory of the anti-semites. They have forced the intellectual and humanist passions of Jews to quit the terrain of speaking for human and legal rights or for searching like Spinoza for some accommodation between faith and reason in order to defend themselves once again from the antisemitism that has taken new forms.

Jews in the end are Semites and when in the Middle East they look like other Semites. Thus antisemitism, although defined as being hostile to Jews, is actually a denial of the right of all those loosely grouped in the category of Semites to lead their own existence. The role of the intellectual and the university is to examine dispassionately the history, politics and possibilities of human advance. There is a major role for universities in Britain, America, Europe, Latin America and Asia to engage with universities in Arab countries and Israel to challenge accepted wisdoms and invite people to see the world differently. Only a tiny handful of books are translated into Arabic. Universities in the Arab world are centres of belief as much as they are places where independent thinking can occur. In turn, too, many campuses in Europe and North America are where people with fixed positions shout at or talk past each other. University leaders, both in the teaching faculty and amongst students, shy away from the obligation to force different positions to meet in debate and intellectual inquiry. There is a great twenty-first-century duty on universities to challenge antisemitism and to allow Muslim and Jewish students to meet, mingle and find points of contact.

In January 2008, the British Government ministry responsible for universities was so concerned at the failure of universities to get to grips with the problem of antisemitism that it had to issue formal guidelines under the heading 'Promoting Good Campus Relations, Fostering Shared Values and Preventing Violent Extremism in Universities and Higher Education Colleges'. The guidelines told universities to:

- Ensure student safety and campuses free from bullying, harassment and intimidation
- Protect and support vulnerable students
- Take responsibility for tackling violent extremism

Having to issue such guidelines to Britain's universities was an admission by government officials of the extent of the problem of antisemitic attacks on the campus. At one level, the British authorities are to be applauded for having recognised what was going on and, at least at the level of government bureaucracy, trying to do something about it. But the very fact that a European government had to intervene to stop anti-Jewish bullying on the campus demonstrates the gravity of the problem. Other nations continue to turn a blind eye in the hope that anitsemitism directed against Jewish university students is just a passing phase, a political moment of excitement and extreme language which many students experience and quickly grow out of. Yet if such language, and at times violent acts, were directed against black or Muslim students, there would be an outcry amongst professors, university staff and students. A double standard applies to young Jews at the universities of Britain, the rest of Europe and North America. This is not imagined, cooked up, or exaggerated as the next chapter will argue.

4

Attacks on Jews

An essential right – call it a civil right, a human right, a right of citizenship, what you will – is to live as free of fear as is possible. For centuries Jews lived in fear. They had no legal rights, even in proud parliamentary democracies like Britain. They could not send their children to university in European countries because Christians demanded limits on the number of Jewish students. When, finally, after the Holocaust, Jews were able to create their tiny state ($\frac{1}{520}$ of the area occupied by Arab nations), even that was contested. The very notion of a Wales-sized Israel – where Jews would never again be second-class citizens and the religious amongst them could follow their faith – was opposed bitterly and by violent hate.

In the first years of the twenty-first century, hundreds of millions in the Euro-Atlantic region and further afield live lives incomparably freer of fear than their parents, grand-parents or remoter ancestors did. With one exception: Jews. Fear has returned as an intimate part of being Jewish in a way that non-Jews can seek to understand but cannot directly experience. Jews in many settled democratic countries have to live with a degree of fear that no other religion, community or birth-defined group has to face. Jewish places of worship are attacked, Jewish cemeteries desecrated, Jewish school-boys and schoolgirls spat at or abused as they go to school. Jewish citizens have to appeal for extra police protection or, in the case of Britain, have to raise millions of pounds to pay for enhanced security for their institutions and events. Jewish university students are singled out for extremist political abuse and sometimes physical assault.

British Jews have an affinity with Israel just as seventeenth- or eighteenth-century Catholics in Britain had an affinity with Rome. Today Israel is singled out for hate campaigns without precedent in our media or political discussion. No British citizen of Arab descent is made to feel responsible for the torture and lack of freedom in Syria or Egypt, or the inhumane treatment of women in Saudi Arabia. Yet British citizens who are Jews are considered responsible for every violation of human rights Israel undertakes or is forced to undertake under the permanent threat of terror and calls for the eradication of Israel from the world map. The journalists' or university teachers' unions call for boycotts of contacts with Jews in Israel. Never would they dream of calling for boycotts of journalists or academics in states whose behaviour makes even the most brutal of Israel's actions seem restrained by comparison. To be sure, the political activists who turn out for local union branch meetings and secure election as delegates to union conferences are not representative of the majority of dues-paying union members. The NUJ executive found a procedural way to dump the mandatory resolution of its 2007 annual delegate meeting where, by a 64–56 vote (out of 40,000 NUJ members), the call for a boycott of Israel was adopted. The union leadership patted itself on the back for defusing a decision that has brought scorn and criticism on its head.

Similarly, the leaders of the university and college teachers' union (UCU) found ways of wriggling out of the anti-Jewish resolution their conference had agreed after taking legal advice. They did so out of a sense of fear – one would hope shame – at the damage caused to the newly merged union, which was subject to worldwide condemnation at the objectively anti-Jewish nature of its boycott call. The UCU has been widely criticised in the House of Commons for its failure to defend Jewish students on university campuses in Britain and its tolerance of extremist groups organising university students, which use language of hate against Jews and Israel no different from that of fascist or Nazi-admiring political groups. UCU activists hostile to working with Jewish academics in Israel did not give up. In May 2008, a tiny handful of union delegates obsessed with their search for an end to contacts with Jews in Israeli universities successfully passed a resolution smearing Jewish professors and lecturers by accusing them of being 'complicit' in the conflict. Although the wording of the union resolution avoided an explicit call for a boycott, it called on British university teachers to consider the moral and political implications of collaborating with Jewish academics in Israel. Thus, of all the academics in all the states in the world, the British university teachers' union singles out Jews in Israel. As in the past, being a Jewish professor is not a comfortable position to hold. And is it a coincidence after the UCU campaign that sadly the level of campus antisemitism was reported to have significantly increased in July 2008?

Antisemitism is taught more as history than current affairs. In each individual country there may be one or two horrific antisemitic attacks in a year, plus low-level assaults, vandalism, jostling and insults. One person knowing I was working on this subject wrote to protest that, as a Jew, he had been pushed and insulted as a schoolboy decades ago and 'So what?' This approach belongs to the good old-fashioned English 'Let's take the rough with the smooth' philosophy.

But in each country we tend only to read about antisemitic incidents that happen and which catch the news editor's eye.

All news is local, then national, and coverage of what happens abroad is – to put it politely – not exactly a speciality of the British press. As for readers of American papers outside of the big east- and west-coast cities, serious international journalism and news coverage of what happens in other countries died long ago. It is possible, however, to construct a year in the life of antisemitism as it impacts through violence against Jews. A very dry but strictly factual publication called *Hate Crimes in the OSCE Region* is published as an annual report by the Warsaw-based Office for Democratic Institutions and Human Rights (ODIHR), which is part of the OSCE – the body set up to bring together communist and non-communist states in Europe and North America in the 1970s. Russia, sadly, is now trying to sabotage the work of the OSCE, which puts great emphasis on monitoring elections and examining freedom-of-expression issues in member states. Moscow regards many of the OSCE member states – or problem regions arising from the break-up of the Soviet Union – as falling within its sphere of influence. Russia resents the role of the OSCE and its human rights body, ODIHR, and their desire to report on how free elections are in all their member states and what is being done to uphold freedom of expression.

The annual hate crimes survey is rigorous and based on fully reported events in different countries. The ODIHR report covering 2006 tells us just how much antisemitic attacks are on the rise across many different countries, but the report does not cover every antisemitic crime and in the diary below I have included other reports. The historian Tony Judt has written the magisterial *Postwar: A History of Europe Since 1945*, which has a fine summary of

Communist antisemitism. 'Stalin was an anti-semite and always had been,' he accurately writes. But Judt, who has spent much of his career in New York, loses his sure-footedness when he dismisses twenty-first-century post-Communist antisemitism in Europe. Writing of more recent European politics he confidently announces: 'Anti-Jewish feelings were largely unknown in contemporary Europe – *except* [my emphasis] among Muslims and especially Europeans of Arab descent.' This statement typecasts Muslim and Arabs as being principally responsible for the fear that Jews experience. But as the list below shows, many of the most obscene and unpleasant instances of antisemitism occur in countries where there is no or only a negligible Muslim or Arab community. To be sure, Judt is right that the type of antisemitism of the late nineteenth century or of the years between the First World War and the Second World War is not in evidence. But dislike and suspicion of, contempt for and violence against Jews is now part of contemporary Europe and Judt does his high and secure reputation little service in downplaying the phenomenon. Let the reader judge if antisemitism is happening or is history.

5 January 2006, Belgium. A man insults and attacks a Jewish couple and their baby on a train to Antwerp. He is arrested.

11 January 2006, Russia. Nine people are stabbed in a Moscow synagogue.

14 January 2006, Canada. A teacher tells his pupils that Jews control the media and that the Holocaust was a media invention.

27 January 2006, Tallinn, Estonia. The Holocaust

monument in Kalevi Lajiva where 6000 Jews were murdered by the Nazis and their collaborators is desecrated.

27 January 2006, France. A Jewish student files a complaint that leads to a four-month suspension of his teacher for an antisemitic remark.

3 February 2006, Ukraine. A man armed with a knife enters the Brodsky synagogue in Kiev shouting 'all Jews should be killed', but is restrained by guards.

8 February 2006, Romania. The Jewish cemetery of Vatra Dorna is desecrated and three tombs vandalised.

13 February 2006, France. A young Jew, Ilan Halimi, previously kidnapped, is found severely injured and dies shortly thereafter. The kidnappers ask for the synagogue to pay to release him because 'all Jews are rich'.

14 and 15 February 2006, Italy. Antisemitic graffiti are daubed on the walls of schools in Milan and Cesena.

19 February 2006, Russia. An Israeli student is assaulted and injured by a group of unknown youths in St Petersburg.

27 February 2006, France. Antisemitic graffiti are daubed on the walls of a school in Sainte-Geneviève des Bois.

27 February 2006, Russia. A swastika is painted on the front door of the Jewish Charity Centre.

February 2006, Iran. Iran's biggest-selling newspaper, *Hamshahri*, organises the 'Holocaust International Cartoon Contest' as a riposte to the cartoons of the Prophet that had been published in a right-wing Danish paper. One thousand antisemitic cartoons from sixty-two countries are sent in and put on display.

February 2006, Italy. An Italian MEP, the secretary-general of the Fiamma Tricolore Party, states in an interview that he has no way of confirming or denying whether gas chambers were used during the Holocaust.

3 and 4 March 2006, France. The son of a rabbi, and later a Jewish man wearing a kippa, are subjected to antisemitic insults in Sarcelles, and are assaulted and injured.

10 March 2006, Canada. A fire occurs at a synagogue, which had already twice been vandalised in February with anti-semitic messages.

25 March 2006, Russia. A group of skinheads follow, attack and beat three students in St Petersburg after they took part in an anti-racism demonstration.

March 2006, Poland. Radio Maryja, with its three million audience, broadcasts a programme in which its commentator accuses Jews of having initiated the 'Holocaust Industry'.

20 April 2006, Ukraine. Two separate attacks on Jewish youngsters take place in Dnipropetrovsk.

20 April 2006, Russia. The Orenburg synagogue is attacked and its windows smashed by fifteen skinheads to mark Adolf Hitler's birthday.

29 April 2006, Russia. Two members of the Russia Parliament address a gathering and make anti-Jewish statements.

May 2006, UK. A motion is passed at the annual conference of NATFHE, the union for college teachers (now merged with the university teachers' union, AUT, to form UCU), calling upon members to boycott all Israeli academics. This was aimed at Jewish academics and students.

11 May 2006, Ukraine. Dnipropetrovsk synagogue's wall is daubed with antisemitic signs.

28 May 2006, Poland. The Chief Rabbi is punched and attacked by a man tied to neo-Nazi organisations.

May 2006, Latvia. A Holocaust memorial soon to be unveiled is vandalised in Rezekne.

3 June 2006, Croatia. Young men wearing Nazi shirts verbally and physically assault the Chief Rabbi.

June 2006, Lithuania. Nineteen gravestones and monuments are smashed in a Jewish cemetery in Suderve, near to Vilnius.

June 2006, Croatia. Members of the Zagreb Jewish community receive antisemitic mail. A student is arrested and charged.

June 2006, Ukraine. A synagogue in Kirovograd is vandalised for the fifth time in 2006.

June 2006, Germany. A public bonfire festival in Pretzien, in Saxony-Anhalt, is transformed into a platform for neo-Nazis, with book-burning and antisemitic chants by around 100 skinheads.

June 2006, United States. Two rural Jewish cemeteries are vandalised in New Jersey.

July 2006, Australia. A Jewish youth centre is attacked in Sydney and two synagogues in Melbourne are vandalised. A rabbi and his family are physically assaulted. Walls in several cities are painted with slogans including 'Jews are the new Nazis' and 'Kill Jews'.

4 July 2006, Belgium. A young ultra-orthodox Jewish student is harassed and beaten by a group of other youngsters.

5 July 2006, Russia. A group of Russian Orthodox extremists attack a group of Jews at the All-Russian Exhibition Centre.

16 July 2006, Ukraine. The memorial dedicated to the victims of the Babi Yar massacre in Kiev is vandalised.

Mid-July 2006, United Kingdom. A group of youngsters insult and throw bricks at Jews in Manchester.

24 July 2006, Canada. Three adults are reported tossing stones at worshippers outside a synagogue in Montreal.

25 July 2006, Belgium. The memorial crypt for the Jewish martyrs of Belgium is severely vandalised in Brussels.

27 July 2006, Azerbaijan. Former interior minister Iskendar Gamidov accuses Jews of owning all the land in northern Azerbaijan and says Washington and Tel Aviv were plotting to take over Azerbaijan after the two countries had occupied Syria and Iran.

28 July 2006, United States. A man opens fire at the Jewish Federation of Greater Seattle. One person is killed and five wounded, including a pregnant woman.

31 July 2006, United Kingdom. A man phones the New-castle synagogue and states that Jewish children are all potential targets after the killings of children in Lebanon.

31 July 2006, United States. Mel Gibson says, 'The Jews are responsible for all the wars in the world.'

August 2006, Italy. At an international friendly football match in Livorno, sixty fans from Croatia form themselves into a human swastika and make Nazi salutes.

1 August 2006, Italy. Swastikas are painted on twenty shops in Rome.

6 August 2006, Denmark. The Copenhagen Jewish school receives an antisemitic threatening letter.

14 August 2006, Ukraine. Three men start insulting and beating an instructor celebrating by singing Israeli songs with a group of trainees the end of a seminar in Kiev.

18 August and 13 September 2006, United Kingdom. The Manchester Jewish cemetery is desecrated with forty-seven gravestones damaged.

22 August 2006, Belgium. An Orthodox Jewish family is harassed by people shouting antisemitic slogans.

24 August 2006, Germany. Fifty extremist members of a neo-Nazi movement gather under the motto 'No peace with Israel! Solidarity with Iran'.

August 2006, Serbia. A group of skinheads harass and beat two Israeli tourists at a rock music festival in Belgrade.

August 2006, United Kingdom. A 13-year-old Jewish girl is attacked and left unconscious in a London bus after she was asked whether she was 'Jewish or English'.

August 2006, Bulgaria. 'Holocaust for the Jews' is shouted by Bulgarian soccer fans at a match against a team from Israel.

September 2006, Russia. A man enters a synagogue in Rostov-on-Don screaming pro-Nazi and antisemitic slogans.

September 2006, Russia. Hooligans attack Israeli football fans in Odessa.

September 2006, Canada. A Molotov cocktail hits an Ortho-dox Jewish boy in Montreal.

11 September 2006, Poland. The Polish government asks

the US to close down an antisemitic website called Redwatch. It gave instructions for antisemitic as well as homophobic violence.

16 September 2006, Lithuania. The Vilnius Jewish cemetery is desecrated and up to 20 tombs smashed and uprooted.

17 September 2006, Norway. The Oslo synagogue is attacked and damaged. Four men are arrested and charged. They are also investigated for possible involvement in plans to blow up the Israeli Embassy.

17 September 2006, England. Playing Manchester United, Arsenal fans chant: 'Send the Jews to Auschwitz'.

18 September 2006, Russia. A Jewish man is beaten up on a crowded street in Odessa.

20 September 2006, Croatia. Pro-Nazi slogans are painted on the walls of a Zagreb Jewish school.

22 September 2006, Russia. Two synagogues and a mosque are vandalised in Khabarovsk and Astrakhan.

23 September 2006, Czech Republic. The Mayor of Prague confirms severe security threat towards the Jewish synagogue at the beginning of the Jewish New Year.

26 September 2006, Russia. The Or Avner Jewish School in Volgograd is attacked by vandals. Windows are smashed, a security guard is injured and antisemitic graffiti, including a swastika, are daubed on the walls.

29 September 2006, Norway. A gunman directs automatic rifle-fire at an Oslo synagogue. Four men are arrested and charged.

September 2006, Germany. 'Gas the Jews', 'Synagogues

must burn again' and 'Auschwitz is back' are chants at a football match in Berlin against the Jewish Maccabi club.

10 October 2006, United Kingdom. An Orthodox Jewish young boy is insulted and attacked by two separate groups of boys.

23 October 2006, Hungary. Hundreds of people shout antisemitic slogans and throw objects at the Great Synagogue in Budapest.

October 2006, Czech Republic. Fifty-five tombs are damaged in a Jewish cemetery in Zamberk.

October 2006, Russia. Holocaust denier and former Ku Klux Klan leader David Duke gives a lecture to mark the publication in Russian of his book *The Jewish Question Through the Eyes of an American* at the private university Inter Regional Academy of Personnel Management (MAUP), which also distributes antisemitic literature and organises anti-Zionist meetings.

October 2006, The Netherlands. 'Hamas. Hamas. Jews to the gas' is chanted by Utrecht fans at a match against Ajax in Utrecht. The Ajax team, rather like Tottenham Hotspur in London, is seen as Jewish.

November 2006, Iran. Following up the 'Holocaust International Cartoon Contest', an organiser, member of the newspaper *Hamshahri* and cited by the *New York Times*, states that the exhibition will 'continue until the destruction of Israel'.

6 November 2006, Hungary. A Jewish school is vandalised in Vác, before further vandal attacks occur on the local synagogue and the Holocaust memorial.

9 November 2006, Germany. A group of neo-Nazis vandalise a *Kristallnacht* memorial monument in Frankfurt hours after the town's annual commemorative ceremony.

9 November 2006, United Kingdom. A synagogue is defaced in south London.

12 November 2006, Belarus. The Yama Holocaust memorial in Minsk is vandalised.

13 November 2006, Switzerland. Antisemitic graffiti are painted on the door of a garage located next to the Beth Habat Jewish School in Geneva.

23 November 2006, France. In the aftermath of a football match between France and Israel, around 150 local fans attack a young French Jew, shouting 'kill the Jews' and other antisemitic slogans. A man dies in the ensuing affray.

26 November 2006, Austria. An intruder smashes windows and breaks other objects in the Lauder Chabad Jewish School in Vienna.

30 November 2006, Belgium. Ten teenagers shout antisemitic slogans and throw stones at a group of Orthodox Jewish students during a school trip in Beringen.

30 November 2006, Belarus. The Jewish memorial monument dedicated to the victims of the Brest Ghetto is damaged.

December 2006, Germany. A 14-year-old Jewish girl from Berlin is granted police protection after being insulted, beaten and humiliated for months by youths on the basis of her faith.

12 December 2006, France. A group of Jewish youngsters

is refused access inside a bus by the driver because of their skullcaps.

15 December 2006, Russia. An incapacitating gas is released by an assaulter at a Hanukkah celebration in a local Jewish community centre in Pskov.

16 December 2006, Ukraine. Three Orthodox Jews are attacked by youngsters screaming antisemitic slogans.

December 2006, Russia. A Molotov cocktail is thrown at the Jewish centre in Ulyanovsk.

December 2006, Iran. The government organises a conference to promote denial of the Holocaust to which leading Jew-haters from across the world are invited as honoured guests of Iran.

December 2006, Russia. An extreme right-wing group organises a rally in front of the Iranian Embassy in Moscow to express solidarity with the president's views on the Holocaust and 'deplore Israeli policies and the world Jewry'.

December 2006, Hungary. A synagogue and a Jewish community centre are defaced with swastikas and Nazi slogans in Pécs.

December 2006, United States. The Beth Israel synagogue in Niagara Falls in New York is repeatedly vandalised and its walls daubed with anti-Jewish messages.

Similar lists could be produced for any year in the twenty-first century. In the United Kingdom, the government has gone further than others in ordering the police to record and treat as serious antisemitic attacks. When the Council of Eur-ope, representing 47 European nations, reported on antisemitism in 2007 it had difficulty in establishing accurate statistics. What is clear is that attacks on Jews are taking place with a greater intensity today than in the decades after 1945. Contrary to the view that antisemitism is linked principally to the conflict in the Middle East, or to the new communities of Muslims in Europe, the evidence shows that white, racist and extreme right-wing or Neo-Nazi propaganda and activity are back at their age-old business of targeting Jews.

5

Languages and Images

This sense of fear that haunts Jews became clearer and clearer as a group of British MPs examined the problem in a report published in 2006. They were told by the Chief Rabbi, Sir Jonathan Sacks: 'If you were to ask me is Britain an anti-semitic society, the answer is manifestly and clearly No. It is one of the least antisemitic societies in the world.' However, the lay leader of British Jews, Henry Grunwald, the president of the Board of Deputies of British Jews, appeared to con-tradict the Chief Rabbi when he said, 'There is probably a greater feeling of discomfort, greater concerns, greater fears now about antisemitism than there have been for many decades.' In fact, both the religious and the lay Jewish leaders were right. Britain is not an antisemitic country. Nor are most of the world's democratic nations or even those semi-democracies like Russia or Venezuela, where antisemitism is visible but society and political leadership as a whole are not gripped by or organised around antisemitism, as is the case in some majority Islamic countries or was the case under Hitler or Stalin in Nazi Germany or Soviet Russia.

The British novelist Howard Jacobson has written of a 'certain grinding low level of antisemitism all Jews learn to live with'. The obvious antisemitic incidents like attacks on rabbis or throwing bricks at synagogue windows are perhaps easy to record. They are on the increase in Britain and across

81

the world. But the MPs concluded that there was a new version of antisemitism that the House of Commons should be concerned about, namely: 'Antisemitism in public and private discourse, for example, the language and tone adopted by the media, political groups, organisations and individuals. These are harder to identify, often go unreported, but are nevertheless extremely significant.'

The new fear amongst Jews comes from the way in which the language used about Jews and Jewishness is being recalibrated. The first reference to 'antisemitism' comes from 1871, when a German populist politician was seeking to whip up feelings against a minority group in the recently united Germany and other German-speaking lands. Jews by then had become integrated and as a community that gave great importance to learning and memory had become visible in some professions, banking and the industries and services filling the consumer needs of the new bourgeoisie. They were not, however, part of the land-owning classes, or the Prussian military, still less the high state service and courtiers around the Kaiser. In late nineteenth-century Germany it was bad form to organise a political campaign against Jews per se when the united Germany was seeking to be a nation giving expression to the values of the *Aufklärung* (Enlightenment) as well as those of Goethe, Kant and Heine rather than the Jew-hatred of medieval or Lutheran Germany. So to give this new politics a more elegant, ethno-scientific patina, the term 'antisemitism' was coined. At a time when English and French imperialisms were defining themselves in racial terms – 'the white man's burden' to quote Kipling – 'antisemitism' converted Christian hostility to Jews into a new politics of ethnic or race superiority.

Today, Jew-haters try to avoid using the term 'Jew'or 'Jewish' and instead reach for the word 'Zionist' or 'Zionism' as a substitute that does not carry the obvious negativity of 'Jew'. Clearly Zionism as a political movement has a political-historical specificity linked to the creation of a Jewish state on the eastern shores of the Mediterranean. Today, anti-semitism and anti-Zionism keep Israel permanently on the defensive, perpetually afraid, never sure when and from where the next onslaught will come. Defensiveness, fear and insecurity are the three worst conditions for successful, generous, tolerant politics. If others like me, non-Jews, want Israel both to survive and become able to make peace with others then a first requirement is to confront modern neo-antisemitism. We now talk of 'hard' and 'soft' power. So too, there is hard and soft antisemitism. My political community – the left, the liberals, the progressives, the pro-Europeans, friends of Palestine, supporters of human rights causes worldwide, modern British and European Muslims, my journalist and trade union friends, the *bien pensants* of Islington, Notting Hill, my fellow MPs of all parties – needs to understand that until neo-antisemitism is confronted, contained and rolled back the chances of movement on the Israel-Palestine question are slim.

Just as antisemitism was a euphemism for anti-Jewish politics, so too is anti-Zionism an attempt to find a formula that covers up a call for the eradication of the state of Israel. And on the whole when a state gets eradicated, its citizens vanish, one way or another. So anti-Zionism is Jew-hatred by other linguistic means. Martin Luther King, who also knew about the nature of fear from the struggle of his own people, had this reply: 'When people criticise Zionists, they mean Jews. You're talking antisemitism.'

It is not an accident that the most notorious of the classic antisemitic documents is called *The Protocols of the Elders of*

Zion [my emphasis]. The double discrediting of Jews and the specific creation of a Jewish state is intended. The British National Party, which yields nothing to the far left in its hatred of Israel, uses Zionists and Zionism as its preferred code for Jews and Jewishness. It cannot be repeated often enough that criticism of unacceptable Israeli behaviour is neither antisemitic nor anti-Zionist. Israel must face the consequences of its actions as a modern democratic state and live with criticism if its politicians or soldiers do things that distress others in the democratic world.

Many who use the term 'Zionist' as an alternative to 'Jewish' will be confident in their own belief that they are not antisemitic but simply using a political, rather than religious or racial adjective. In his poem, 'Killed in Crossfire', Tom Paulin referred to the 'Zionist SS' to express his anger and anguish at the behaviour of Israeli troops. Paulin's language on Israel is extreme. Interviewed for the Cairo paper *Al Ahram*, the Irish poet and Oxford don said of Jewish settler immigrants into Israel from the USA, 'They should be shot dead. I think they are Nazis, racists. I feel nothing but hatred for them.' Paulin, I think and hope, could never have written 'Jewish SS' to make his point, but he thought he was on safer linguistic territory by using 'Zionist'. Jonathan Freedland, the journalist and novelist, sought to chide Paulin and his lines about the 'Zionist SS'.

First, they are hyperbolic: no matter how bad Israel is, it is not the Third Reich. Second, they seem designed to cancel out the world's empathy for Jewish suffering in the 1930s and 1940s: under this logic, the Holocaust has now been 'matched' by Israeli misbehaviour, therefore the Jews have forfeited any claim they might once have had to special understanding. The world and the 'Jews' are now even. Third, and worse, the

Nazi-Zionist equation does not merely neutralise memories of the Holocaust – it puts Jews on the wrong side of them . . . Jews end up with the gravest hour in their history first taken from them – then returned with themselves cast as villains rather than victims. If anti-Zionists wonder why Jews find this antisemitic, perhaps they should imagine the black reaction if the civil rights movement – or any other vehicle of black liberation – was consistently equated with white slave traders of old. It feels like a deliberate attempt to find a people's rawest spot – and tear away at it.

The objection may be made that Jonathan Freedland, as a Jew, would say that, wouldn't he? But in a liberal, open society the question is rather why does a line in a poem cast fear into the heart of British citizens who happen to be Jews? Anti-Jewish images, some of them going back to medieval stereotypes, have resurfaced. In 2003, a British paper, the *Independent*, ran a cartoon of the former Israeli prime minister Ariel Sharon stuffing a Palestinian baby into his mouth while wearing a fig leaf saying 'Vote Likud'. Sharon has much to answer for in terms of innocent blood spilled as a result of his military and political orders. And cartoons, from Gillray's obscene depictions of eighteenth-century politicians and royalty to the Danish caricatures of the Prophet Mohammed, are meant to offend. Yet a core antisemitic image is of Jews killing children to use their blood in rituals. And far from there being a shudder of distaste at the newspaper's invocation of the centuries-old blood libel of the child-devouring Jew, the cartoon was given first prize by a jury in the annual competition of the British Political Cartoon Society.

The year before – 2002 – the *New Statesman* had on its front page a Star of David impaling a supine Union Jack. The cover-page headline was 'A Kosher Conspiracy?' The Star of

David was gold rather than blue. The symbol of Jewishness stabbing a prostrate Union Jack was a classic pre-1939 image of wealthy Jews being disloyal to their country of citizenship.

The *Guardian* in 2006 published a long essay-feature, which compared Israel to apartheid South Africa. I spent much time in South Africa in the 1980s working with the independent, black trade-union movement, which was the spearhead inside the country of the struggle against apartheid. I lay in ditches outside townships as apartheid troop carriers rumbled by. I sat in hotels or walked on beaches denied to my black comrades. Arabs in Israel can travel in the same buses as Jews, swim off the same beaches, study at the same universities and join visitors from Europe for a drink in a hotel. The South African anti-apartheid campaigners, after a brief flurry of armed resistance, took the road of Gandhi, Mandela and Martin Luther King and opted for peaceful organisation against the white minority rulers. Many Jewish leftists in South Africa worked as organisers for the black workers and their unions. Jewish lawyers, journalists and intellectuals made the case to their fellow whites for an end to apartheid. The language against apartheid was directed against the ideology not against the white race.

There would be no greater impetus to peace in the Middle East than learning from South Africa. The Palestinians and the Middle East's Jew-hating political leaders should look to Nelson Mandela and the alliance for democracy and justice between Jews and blacks in the former land of apartheid. True, there is a politics of supremacism in the Middle East, but it is practised by those who denounce the right of Jews to live in the state where they were born. The lessons from South Africa are the very opposite of those advanced by the *Guardian*. It is the racism of antisemitic supremacy that should be confronted or the appalling treatment of minorities in countries like Saudi Arabia or Iran, among others. Jews in Israel will travel on their buses with anyone – all they ask is that they are not blown up.

In July 2006, the *Guardian* published an image of a mailed fist with Stars of David smashing into a bloodied child's face, as Israeli soldiers sought to defeat and disarm the Hezbollah militants who used Lebanon as a base to attack Jews. The bombing of Lebanon and the deaths of hundreds of Lebanese civilians inflamed anti-Israeli opinion worldwide. But the *Guardian*'s use of Stars of David trampling on others was an image straight out of Nazi-era propaganda posters, showing Jewish influence over Europe. In December 1941, the Reich Propaganda Department of the Nazi Party published its weekly wall-poster newsletter called *Parole der Woche*. Under the heading 'The Jewish Conspiracy', it showed Stars of David at the heart of a network of Jewish influence and power. The *Guardian* apologised saying the point the cartoon was making might have been interpreted as 'implicating Judaism rather than the Israeli government in the present conflict'. The *Guardian* however was in good company. The Conservative MP Sir Peter Tapsell said that Israel's action in Lebanon was 'reminiscent of the Nazi atrocity on the Jewish quarter of Warsaw'. Sir Peter, a veteran Tory right-winger, was not alone. The Russian propagandist Mikhal Nazarov also responded to the Israeli-Hezbollah conflict by calling it 'another unpunished riot of the Judeo-Nazi state of Israel'. In December 2006, buildings in the university suburbs of Boston, including Cambridge and Brookline, were plastered with poster cartoons describing life in occupied Palestine as identical to the Warsaw Ghetto and demanding the abolition of Israel. Further away in Brazil, the Tapsell world view was supported by the Federal Congresswoman Socorro Gomes, who used the term 'Nazi-Zionists' to describe Israel. Sir Peter from the parliamentary right in Britain thus joins Ms Gomes, a Communist in the Congress of Brazil, in equating Israelis with Nazis.

The *Daily Telegraph* printed a cartoon showing two identically wrecked cities – 'Warsaw 1943' and 'Tyre 2006'. The Lebanese campaign in 2006 was a disaster for Israel, and a victory for Hezbollah in terms of public opinion. More than a thousand perished in the fighting, missile attacks and air raids. But to compare the four-week military engagement in Lebanon in 2006 (which also saw hundreds of thousands of Israeli Jews hiding in bomb shelters as missiles fired by Hezbollah, but provided by Syria and Iran, rained down on civilian targets) to the systematic, organised massacre of Jews in Poland and the destruction of the Warsaw Ghetto in 1943 is to create a nexus that reeks even as it plays into the hands of antisemites seeking to establish an equivalence between Israel and the Third Reich.

Again, the idea that the editors of the *Guardian*, *Independent*, *Daily Telegraph* or *New Statesman* are deliberately or even semi-consciously antisemitic is absurd. But slowly, unwittingly, they are sucked into seeing the Jews of the state of Israel, and by extension, Jews in Britain or other countries who support the existence of Israel, in terms that echo the classic evocations of traditional antisemitism. One of the most popular high-brow best-sellers of recent years was Jostein Gaadner's *Sophie's World*. In 2006 he published an article in the main Norwegian paper, *Aftenposten*. Titled 'God's Chosen People', it argued that Israel and Jews see themselves as a special case, a 'Chosen People' who are allowed to behave without moral restraint. Israel, concluded the author, did not have the right to exist. There is no country in Europe which has done more to promote a global politics of peace, reconciliation and tolerance than Norway. So for a well-known Norwegian to deny to Jews born over generations in Israel their right to their state comes as a shock. It is an important reminder that twenty-first-century neo-antisemitism is not a product of Islamist ideology but has its roots in European *mentalités*. However, contemporary Islamism has taken classic European antisemitism and created a new monster which we must now examine.

6

The Ideological Basis

This interview was broadcast on Egyptian TV in May 2002:

INTERVIEWER DUAA AMER: 'What's your name?'

BASMALLAH: 'Basmallah.'

AMER: 'How old are you, Basmallah?'

BASMALLAH: 'Three and a half.'

AMER: 'Basmallah, do you know the Jews?'

BASMALLAH: 'Yes.'

AMER: 'Do you like them?'

BASMALLAH: 'No.'

AMER: 'Why don't you like them?'

BASMALLAH: 'Because.'

AMER: 'Because they are what?'

BASMALLAH: 'They are apes and pigs.'

AMER: 'Because they are apes and pigs. Who said that about them?'

BASMALLAH: 'Our God.'

AMER: 'Where did he say that about them?'

BASMALLAH: 'In the Koran.'

Uncomfortable as it may be for progressives who have worked for harmony between races and religions, the question of modern neo-antisemitism cannot be divorced from the contemporary crisis of Islam. In 1989 the scholar and writer specialising in Islam, Malise Ruthven, investigated the response of British Muslims to the publication of Salman Rushdie's book *The Satanic Verses*. It followed Iranian Ayatollah Khomeini's fatwa calling for the death of Rushdie. Like Voltaire's *Candide*, Ruthven goes as a friend of Islam and explores gently the contradictions in the position taken by British Muslims over Rushdie's novel. In an hilarious encounter at a demonstration against *The Satanic Verses*, Ruthven gently explains to a man who denounces the novel as 'totally filthy' that there are many books in public circulation that say much more insulting things about Islam and the Prophet Mohammed. He quotes text from Dante in which Mohammed is placed in the eighth circle of hell where he suffers the perpetual torment of having his intestines, liver and anus cut and recut as he writhes in agony. His interlocutor has never heard of Dante, but he does know that the Jews somehow are involved in the affair. As Ruthven points out that the fatwa and the protests had turned a difficult and complicated novel into a global best-seller, which every thinking person had to read to see what all the fuss was about, his new acquaintance gave up the argument. 'We Muslims don't think in materialistic terms like the Jews you know,' as if any mention of money and the huge sales the book would have was somehow linked to Jews.

As he explored his theme and visited Bradford, talking to many of the people involved in the campaign against Rushdie, Ruthven, who it needs to be stressed is an Islamophile, came to make a startling comparison when he wrote:

Islamic fundamentalism, like fascism, holds out the vision of a 'fully integrated' society free from damaging divisions of class and wealth – a society which is presumed to have existed in the golden age before Western colonialism entered the picture . . . Like fascism, it seeks a psychological foundation in absolute certainty: the only difference being that instead of the Will of the Leader, it relies on the Will of God as imparted through His representatives on earth or as revealed in His Book.

I do not like the term 'Islamofascism', because it is wrong to confuse a religion with an ideology or a political practice. But it is important to note that Ruthven was making the comparison as an Islamophile long before it came into fashionable use by American neo-conservatives after 9/11.

Ruthven also detected something more worrying. 'Embedded in the generalised anti-Western thrust of fundamentalist discourse there exists a specific antisemitic threat.' He relates this to a core element in Islamic fundamentalism.

The fundamentalist mentality – absolutist, anti-democratic and highly authoritarian – is prone to see conspiracies where none exist . . . The conspiracy theory – of which the anti-Jewish version is one of the archetypes – had some plausibility in the absence of rational explanations. Jews were prominent in publishing; Jews supported the Israeli occupation of Muslim lands. Ergo, *The Satanic Verses* was part of some wider movement directed against Islam.

A Bradford Muslim, Liaqat Hussein, told Ruthven that there was 'an anti-Islamic lobby throughout the Western world, spearheaded by the Jews. You only have to look at the statement of writers supporting Rushdie,' said Hussein. 'Almost a third of them are Jews.' When Ruthven pointed out that many secular Jewish writers like Susan Sontag, Norman Mailer or Philip Roth had supported Rushdie for the simple reason that book-burning and blasphemy laws were against everything they believed in and that, if anything, religious Jews in Britain had sought to express some understanding of Muslim outrage, he failed to convince his Bradford friend. 'That they would suspect a plot, a conspiracy of malignant forces ranged against Islam was, I suppose, inevitable. In a sense it flattered Muslim self-esteem that Islam should be the target of such a conspiracy, whether organised by Jews in revenge for Muslim resistance in Palestine or by Christians carrying on the crusades.'

When Ruthven wrote down those words nearly two decades ago, antisemitism, if it was considered a problem at all in British politics, was still associated with the far right. To be sure, there was unceasing criticism of Israel, especially over the disastrous occupation and war of attrition in Lebanon, which for many recalled Talleyrand's remark to Napoleon, 'It was worse than a crime, it was an error.' The first Intifada was under way, but the political discourse of the time left little room for antisemitism. Since then, politics has been transformed by the rise of political Islamism, which has imported into Britain the violently antisemitic discourse of Islamist movements like the Muslim Brotherhood or Mawdudi's Jamaat-e-Islami.

Writing lies at the core of neo-antisemitism, and to understand the deep wells of twenty-first-century antisemitism a reading of the core texts is vital. This can be hard work. One of the ideologues of modern Islamist jihadism is Abou Moussab al-Souri, a Syrian Islamist who was allowed to carry on his activities in London in the 1990s by successive home secretaries and their advisers, including a young Conservative activist, David Cameron. Souri has written a 1,600-page *Appeal to World Islamic Resistance*, divided into nine volumes. Souri in turn was inspired and extensively quotes the writings of the Islamist ideologue Sayyid Qutb. The Egyptian Qutb's writings are the most remarkable expression of hate and hostility to Jews ever written in any language in modern times. After Hasan al-Banna, the founder of the Muslim Brotherhood, Qutb is the most important writer of the Egyptian-based global Islamist organisation. He was cruelly put to death by Nasser in 1966 and was transformed from an anti-democratic man of hate into a martyr for Islamist antisemitism.

The founder of the Muslim Brotherhood, Hasan al-Banna, had placed death at the heart of his philosophy.

> The Muslim Community which excels in the art of death and knows how to die the noble death will receive from Allah the greatest life in this world and eternal pleasure in the next. Nothing degrades us more than love of this world and fear of death. So call yourselves to a great effort and strive after the death which will give you life. Know that death can only come once. If you attain it in Allah's path (i.e. *jihad*), that will be your profit in this world and your reward in the next.

This core text of the suicide bomber, the exaltation of being killed in following 'Allah's path' of jihad, has never been repudiated by succeeding Muslim Brotherhood ideologues and preachers. Current Muslim Brotherhood leaders in Egypt play with words. They denounce terrorism but allow their favourite imams to justify terrorist killing of Jewish women and children in Israel on the grounds that the boys might become Israeli soldiers. They insist that sharia law with its denial of major democratic rights would not be applied if they won government power in Egypt, but later on once economic and social problems had been solved. However, Dr Mohammed Abdul Bari, the general secretary of the Muslim

Council of Britain, when asked if he approved of stoning women to death for adultery replied, 'It depends on the circumstances.' His No. 2, Inayat Bunglawala, also refused to condemn stoning. As he told a London audience, 'a woman was stoned to the death during the lifetime of the Prophet so you are asking me to condemn my prophet'.

Sayyid Qutb would not have quarrelled with these sentiments. However, it is Qutb's obsessive hate for Jews in his book *Our Struggle with the Jews* that places him on a par with European Jew-haters whose politics of killing Jews culminated in the Nazi years. Qutb is now a household word well beyond his Islamist followers. Hans Küng, the German theologian and historian of religion, sees Qutb as a key figure in the Islamist renewal. In his study *Islam: Past, Present and Future*, Professor Küng asks:

> Is a new age also dawning for Islam, for a world religion which now hopes to make a great breakthrough in the southern hemisphere and become the greatest religion in the world in the new millennium – with more than one billion Muslims at the beginning of the millennium? Is Islam the heir to Christianity which, as a consequence of its compromise with colonialism and imperialism and the social development towards individualism and secularism, has lost its credibility in southern lands? Whether these are dreams or not, the West is confronted with an Islamic renewal which has many aspects
>
> • The re-Islamisation of the Muslim states
> • An intensification of the Muslim mission in Africa and Asia
> • And the activation of the Muslim minorities in Western states.

According to Küng, 'Renewal always takes place through a return to the foundations of Islam, Qu'ran and Sunnah (the tradition of the Prophet)' and Qutb from Egypt stands alongside the Indian Muslim ideologue Mawdudi and Iran's Ali Shari'ati as the leader of the renewal movement in Islam. The three men, notes Küng, who notoriously had his own difficulties with his own religious superiors in the Vatican on account of his independent thinking, 'reject . . . reason, rationality and science'. Qutb's passion and his flowing journalistic style can be seen in his book *Milestones*, which can be bought in many Muslim bookshops in London. A quick click on Google opens the way to reading *Milestones* on scores of well-organised sites aimed at Muslims or those interested in Islam. It is, to be honest, a long and rambling read, full of quotes from the Koran with interlinked commentaries.

Writers like Martin Amis and the politician Michael Gove, who have quoted Qutb in their books on Islamism, have made much of Qutb's visit to the Midwest of the United States between 1948 and 1950. Born in 1906, Qutb became, in 1939, a civil servant in the Ministry of Education in Cairo. After the Allied unity of the Second World War changed to the ideological confrontation-containment struggle with communism, the United States launched an ambitious programme of scholarship and sponsored visits hoping to win friends and influence people in the Muslim world, at a time when the US was supporting national movements against colonial rule in North Africa. Thus Qutb was able to study at the Colorado State College of Education and receive a diploma there. Far from winning this influential Islamist ideologue and activist to support Western democracy and liberal values, Qutb was appalled by what he saw in the conservative Midwest. Back in Egypt he denounced the brutality of the Western materialism and individuality he had experienced.

Two themes predominate: sex and race. 'The American girl

is well acquainted with her body's seductive capacity. She knows it lies in the face, and its expressive eyes and thirsty lips. She knows seductiveness lies in the round breasts, the full buttocks, and in the shapely thighs, sleek legs – and she knows all this and does not hide it.' Worse than women, for Qutb, were African-Americans and their music: 'Jazz . . . is created by Negroes to satisfy their love of noise and to whet their sexual desires' proclaimed Qutb. This ferocious Puritanism would have made sense to many a sixteenth- or seventeenth-century religious fanatic seeking to find salvation on earth through complete submission to the will of God; a fanatic who tends, on the whole, to be patriarchal, authoritarian and obsessed with the threat of women and sexuality. Qutb insisted on a return to a world in which all rules came direct from God. In his view, the true world of Islam existed nowhere save in the early years of the Prophet's rule. His Egypt, as well as other Arab countries and, of course, the West, lived in a state of ignorance that existed before Islam and the arrival of sharia law. This non-Islamic world of fake Muslims, Christians, Jews and non-believers was *jahiliyyah* and it had to be challenged and overthrown by 'physical power and Jihad'. The secular Arabists like Nasser, Ba'athists in Syria and Iraq, and the liberation nationalists in Algeria and Tunisia (where the American trade union federation had backed the Tunisians in the 1950s against the occupying French) were all part of *jahiliyyah* and had to be fought against, eradicated as jihad emerged victorious and replaced by the gleaming cities on the Islamic hill.

Such millenarianist denunciations and appeals to follow a shining path to the true life of submission, to a power which cannot be challenged, are of course commonplace throughout history. But Qutb's fervour, which in a more mature political environment might have branded him a crank, found

97

resonance in Nasser's Egypt where corruption, brutality and widespread torture and executions of his opponents alienated many. More important, Qutb offered his readers and his followers in the Muslim Brotherhood and other Islamist groups an even more tempting enemy; an enemy whose very existence helped explain the continuing hold of *jahiliyyah* on the world and in the minds of Muslims. That enemy was, and for the millions of Qutb readers today remains, the Jew.

To understand the strength of today's neo-antisemitism, it is necessary to study Qutb's most coherent and argued-through essay-length book, *Our Struggle with the Jews*, which depicts Jews as the mortal enemy of Muslims, indeed of humanity.

> The Jews feel that they are a group cut off from the tree of life, and they just wait for humanity to meet with disaster. They harbour hatred for others. Thus they suffer the punishment due those who hate and bear rancour. Consequently, they make others suffer those same punishments repeatedly, in the form of dissensions among peoples and war which the Jews themselves foment in order to make profits from them. Through these wars and disturbances they cultivate their continuing hatred [for others] and the destructiveness which they impose on people and which others impose on them . . . All of this evil arises only from their own destructive egoism.

In contrast to those who seek words in the Koran that imply some acceptance of Jews, or those who look kindly on the medieval period when Jews and Arabs coexisted on the Iberian peninsula (though with non-Muslims having distinctly inferior status, a point often obscured by writers trying to find harmony and togetherness in past centuries),

Qutb's reading of the Holy Book says the Jews were worse than other groups who worshipped different gods before the arrival of Islam: 'The enmity of the Jews towards the Muslims was always stronger, crueller and deeper in its persistence, and of longer duration, than was the enmity of the poly-theists.'

For Qutb, someone – he suggested Hitler – would arise to punish the Jews whenever they refused to submit. In the be-ginning of Islam:

The Muslims expelled them [the Jews] from the Arabian peninsula . . . Then the Jews again returned to their evil-doing and consequently Allah sent against them others of His servants, until the modern period. Then Allah brought Hitler to rule over them. And once again today the Jews have returned to evil-doing, in the form of 'Israel' which made the Arabs, the owners of the Land, taste of sorrow and woe. So let Allah bring down upon the Jews people who will mete out on them the worst kind of punishment.

Using language and metaphors that are today believed and repeated by millions, Qutb insisted that Jews were involved in a giant – but secret – conspiracy against Islam. 'This Jew-ish consensus [on destroying Islam] would never be found in a pact or open conference. Rather it is like the [secret] agree-ment of one Zionist agent with another on the important goal, as something fundamental.' There can be no peace between Muslim and Jews: 'This is a war which has not been extin-guished, even for one moment, for close on fourteen cen-turies, and which continues until this moment, its blaze raging in all corners of the earth.'

Qutb was writing in the early 1950s for an Egyptian and wider Arab audience that had seen its armies unable to destroy the infant Jewish state after it was set up by the UN. Muslim Brotherhood activists had sent militants to fight against Israel. For Islamists like Qutb, the defeat of the Arabs was not a moment to reject jihad and the killing of Jews and, instead, turn to political or diplomatic solutions, but rather a reflection on the insufficient commitment to Islamism. Qutb rejected the nationalist secularism of Nasser and other Arab anti-colonialists. His call was to place faith in faith and the Jews would be defeated and Israel disappear: 'Today the struggle has indeed become more deeply entrenched, more intense and more explicit, ever since the Jews came from every place and announced they were establishing the state of Israel . . . Nothing will curb their greed short of Islam's defeating them.'

Plunging into Qutb's antisemitic diatribes is to enter a world of unremitting hate against Jews. Qutb returned again and again to anti-Jewish themes. The Jews

> use tricks to infiltrate and use intelligent words to sow doubt and division . . . they have to be seen as traitors, people who don't keep their word, fake friends, hypocrites, friends of bad Muslims. Marx, Freud, Durkheim and Bergson are all Jews who created materialist thinking, atheism, sexualness, Darwinism. They destroy what is holy and moral.

Qutb's attack on Jews was one of many essays that appeared in Egypt in the 1950s. In 1970, the Saudi authorities published the essay as a separate book, collecting some of Qutb's writings under the title *Our Struggle with the Jews*. For good measure, the Saudi editor added references to *The Protocols of the Elders of Zion* in order to buttress some of Qutb's antisemitic ravings. Qutb, for example, anticipates Edward Said's denunciation of 'Orientalism'. Qutb writes that: 'The Jews have instilled men and regimes [in the Islamic world], in order to conspire against this [Muslim] Community. Hundreds, then, even thousands were plotting within the Islamic world, continuing [to appear] in the form of Orientalists and the students of Orientalists [who are] manufactured by Zionism.' The Saudi editor added a reference to the tenth protocol of the Elders of Zion, which describes how Jews will control politicians to do their bidding. He also seeks to support Qutb's case of eternal enmity between Muslim and Jews by quoting the fourth protocol from the legendary forgery: 'We shall never permit the existence of any religion other than our own. For this reason, it is necessary for us to destroy all [other] systems of belief. The decisive result of this will be the deserved fruits of the heretics.'

We now enter a circular world in which *The Protocols of the Elders of Zion* is used as evidence and source material to bolster the case against Jews. The Saudi government has close relations with Western democracies. Had any Communist regime, European government or Asian authorities, or perhaps some odious tyrant like Robert Mugabe or Augusto Pinochet, published Qutb's Jew-hating diatribes then the heavens would have fallen in. But our moral sensibilities have become so blunted that Qutb's writings are widely available and he is treated by commentators as a serious Islamist philosopher. If some pro-Nazi party started to use similar language about Jews or sought to publish the anti-Jewish hates from one of the Nazi antisemites then we would react swiftly and take condign action. Calls for the destruction of Jews from Qutb, however, are treated differently.

Thanks to Ed Husain and his remarkable book *The Islamist*, we now have a clear picture of the centrality of antisemitism at the heart of Islamist thinking and activity in Britain in the 1990s. Ed (the shortened form of his name

Mohammed) Husain went through the different Islamist organisations much as many a young radical student passes
through periods of membership and activism in Trotskyist or
anti-globalisation movements. Having quit Hizb ut-Tahrir,
Husain searched for a less messianic, or in his case the adjective would presumably be Caliphatic, organisation to join
and came across the Islamic Society of Britain. There he
met Inayat Bunglawala, who later rose to prominence as the
spokesman for the Muslim Council of Britain. Other new
comrades in the ISB included Abdurahman Jafar, who later
became a leading member of the Respect Party. When Oona
King defended her parliamentary seat of Bethnal Green
against the Respect Party candidate, George Galloway, in the
2005 General Election she claimed that material was circulated drawing attention to the fact that she had a Jewish
mother as well as an African-American father (see page 23).
Husain was invited to the home of a Palestinian called Abu
Luqman in east London.

> Abu Luqman's deep and powerful hatred of . . . Jews was
> unmistakable. Many times he promised destruction of the
> state of Israel and the return of Muslim control of the
> Holy Land. I sat there and accepted this . . . neither Inayat
> [Bunglawala] nor myself questioned any of this. Jew-bashing
> was an acceptable part of the Islamist curriculum.

Husain continues in a revelatory passage that every young
Muslim and every Israel-hater in England would do well to
read.

> I should have known better. By then I had studied the history
> of Jews in Europe, the progroms, the rejection, the Holocaust.
> I should have spoken out but I didn't. Instead, I was now

leading a different kind of double life. Among Islamists I was a 'brother'. I was not to dispute our unquestioned perceptions: hatred of Jews, Hindus, Americans, Gays, the subordination of women . . . every Wednesday night Inayat would pick me up and drop me off after a session of Koran recitation, religious discussion, antisemitism.

Husain's book describes his attempts to come to terms with his faith while seeking a way to escape from the clutches of the Islamist organisations grouped in the Muslim Council of Britain. He went first to Syria and then to Saudi Arabia to improve his Arabic. In Jeddah he heard for himself the full force of Wahhabi Jew-hatred.

All the mosques had state funded preachers . . . almost without exception, Friday sermons were highly politicised and radical. The Imams prayed for Jihad in Iraq and Palestine to continue, and called on God to destroy the Jews . . . This mantra of destruction would have elicited an Amen from me a decade earlier. Now I sat mute, not even raising my hands as is Muslim custom, but looking around bewildered. How could we? Why did we not learn from the fact that despite Islamist prayers for destruction over five decades, Israel was still in place and America reigned supreme? Was God not telling us something in rejecting Islamist-Wahhabi prayers of cataclysm?

And Husain has little time for the claims of the antisemites that they attack Zionism, but not Jews: 'Islamist apologists point out that they are not against Jews, but Zionists. But . . . this was only a play on words, a shallow trick to pre-empt accusations of antisemitism. To them, Jew and Zionist are synonyms, selectively used to win over a given audience.' In

Saudi Arabia, Husain assiduously attended his classes and courses: 'What I was taught in clandestinely Islamist mosques and cell meetings in Britain was being taught openly at universities in Saudi Arabia. Islamist extremism was nowhere near subsiding.' He felt let down by his teachers.

Islamists of various shades (including Wahhabis and Jihadis) are masters at blaming the Zionists, the Jews, the British, French and Italian imperialists, the Turks and the Freemasons but never themselves . . . What happened to the Muslims? I lamented. Once producers of great thinkers, grammarians, theologians, scientists, innovators, poets, jurists, and architects, today's Muslim schools and universities are producing government-fearing sycophants or extremist zealots. Where are the free thinking intellectuals?

He made friends with a young Saudi couple who had worked in London. Husain and his wife and their new friends dined shortly after the Islamist bombing of the London Underground. Husain innocently asked him whether he thought the nature of education in Saudi schools might have influenced the thinking of the fifteen Saudis who took part in the attacks on New York on 9/11. His new Saudi friend replied instantly, 'No. No, because Saudis were not behind 9/11. The plane hijackers were not Saudi men. 1,246 Jews were absent from work on that day and there is the proof that they, the Jews were behind the killings. Not Saudis.'

Reading Husain took me straight back to my conversation in South Yorkshire with Muslim friends and the willingness almost instantly after the 9/11 atrocities for these decent members of the British Muslim community to defy logic and truth (see page 152). They swallowed whole the myth of the Jews who did not report for work in order to avoid being killed in the Twin Towers, and believed that Mossad had actually organised the attack. Husain four years later had the same reaction: 'It was the first time I heard so precise a number of Jewish absentees. I sat there pondering on the pan-Arab denial of the truth, a refusal to accept that the Wahhabi Jihadi terrorism festering in their midst had inflicted calamities on the entire world.'

Another young British citizen trying to come to grips with Islamism in the same period is the writer and journalist Jason Burke. After university he went to Afghanistan in the early 1990s and spent the next decade travelling through different Muslim communities, trying to make sense of the local politics. In his book *Al-Qaeda: The True Story of Radical Islam* Jason Burke emphasises the centrality of Jew-hate as a mobilising force for Bin Laden. 'That the West and the Jews want to maintain the Islamic world in a state of weakness, division and poverty is taken as a given. Bin Laden ignores the Islamic injunction for tolerance towards the "People of the Book".' Burke goes on to quote Bin Laden's declaration of war, which claims 'that the people of Islam have suffered from aggression, iniquity and injustice imposed on them by the Zionist-crusaders alliance and their collaborators'. In his more personal and autobiographical account of his attempts to come to grips with Islamism – *On the Road to Kandahar* – Burke argues that we should see Islamist antisemitism as deriving from both left and right traditions and European politics.

Many of the radical Muslim groups set up in the 1970s and 1980s made no secret of the fact that they had learned their tactics and organisation from the left, and a surprising number of Islamic militants had actually flirted with left-wing activism before becoming involved in religious radical movements. There was also the antisemitism that marked much left-wing and all radical Islamic thought.

Burke wonders whether the endless number of Islamist activists and militants he had interviewed in his decade of investigation 'might have been radical left-wing activists if the collapse of the Soviet block and the triumph of Western, liberal, democratic free market capitalism had not discredited communism, leaving them with no other ideology or language of opposition to the West beyond that of radical Islam.' Burke is on to something important here. At any stage in modern history there is a market need for a politics that offers a complete transformation of human existence, if only we follow its precepts. The offer to create a new world free of conflict, with all submitting to one overarching will, was central for both communism and fascism. As we know, both totalising ideologies made scapegoats of Jews. Among the many similarities between Hitler and Stalin, antisemitism was the most striking. Burke continues:

There was much too that radical Islamic militants, though they would undoubtedly have denied it, shared with ultra-right-wing ideologies, particularly those that had gripped half of the population of Europe in the middle of the 20th century. There were parallels in terms of the social groups from which the leaders were drawn, there was the common antisemitism and the similar traditions of martyrdom. Then there was also the snarling association of modernity with mediocrity or degeneracy, an insistence on morality and racial or religious purity, an appeal to a mythic past imagined as a perfect era of stability and firm values.

Burke is also right to point out that both communism and fascism arose at a time of immense economic dislocation with new forms of production transforming people's experiences. Settled and stable communities suddenly had to confront poverty as the established means of production disappeared, replaced by foreign imports or relocations of national capital to other parts of the world. Depressingly, he concludes that it took the best part of a century to wind down the attractiveness of communism and fascism, though both ideologies still have their followers. Will it take a further century before radical Islamism runs out of breath as Muslims around the world realise that terror and violence and the ideologies that sanction them are dead ends?

If Burke's timescale is right, then we are seeing a crescendo of antisemitism rather than a new climax. The continuing failure of the intellectual and liberal left in Europe and North America to confront and take on neo-antisemitism or even accept that it is real and a menace to every value that the liberals and the left have ever stood for, will confirm Burke's pessimistic time line. The intolerant right, with their invocation of national identity and their contempt for ideas of international law and supranational governance, play directly into the hands of the antisemitic Islamists. Antisemitism in one country does not exist. It is international. The European Parliament, for example, will not be able to uproot the antisemitic thinking of some of its MEPs until the rest of Europe takes antisemitism seriously. The United States will not be seen as a serious actor against antisemitism until it joins in the common search for new energy policies, which reduce dependence on the Saudi oil that finances the export of Wahhabist antisemitism.

Yet politicians of the right in Britain have nothing but contempt for the need for European cooperation. The American right, and I include protectionist and isolationist Democrats as well as Republicans, are adamant that America does not have to join in international treaties and legally binding obligations to reduce US addiction to Saudi petrol. Fighting neo-antisemitism is not simply a matter of denouncing its more vocal preachers and practitioners, still less trying to attack any expression of hostility to Israel. Neo-antisemitism is rooted in an intellectual failure to understand and describe it adequately, and then draw the necessary conclusions about changes in government policy. It cannot be fought only on the campuses of one nation or by changing the laws of another. It requires a new politics of tolerance and inter-nationalism, which demands new thinking about how we relate one to another as men and women, believers and unbelievers. It needs to address how nations interact, one to another, in a world where national borders, national laws and the agents of government provide little protection against menaces that are transnational in origin and pay no attention to flags or borders.

7

Antisemitism or Antizionism?

Matzo of Zion is the title of a book by Mustafa Tlass, long-serving Syrian defence minister, published in 1983. It repeats the libel that Damascus Jews killed Catholic priests to use their blood to bake matzos – the unleavened bread used during Passover. The book was on sale at the Damascus International Book Fair in 2002.

Each manifestation of neo-antisemitism can be teased out and discussed in its own terms, but for an ideology to sink roots it must claim to reveal the 'invisible' hands or the 'alienation' that are responsible for the way people live and act. For an ideology to command widespread support, it must relieve people of the responsibility for managing their own destiny and instead invite them, as 'victims', to throw in their lot with an unquestioning interpretation, obeying the rules rigorously. An ideology must explain history and show why the adherents of the ideology have the keys to control the next stages in historical development.

Antisemitism is too easily dismissed as archaic prejudice. Physical assaults and abuse of Jews are the most obvious manifestation of antisemitism. Such racist criminality is reprehensible and with tough political or police action can be repressed. But neo-antisemitism is a developed, coherent and organised system of modern politics that has huge influence on the minds of millions. Neo-antisemitism impacts on world politics today like no other ideology. Debate rages in most key world institutions and leading governments on what response to take to pressing problems. More soldiers are actively fighting and dying in different parts of the world than at any time since the classic twentieth-century wars. People movement not seen in centuries gives rise to the transfer of scores of millions from the land of their birth to foreign countries. New states are being created. New international institutions, many with executive authority like the WTO, Nato, the IMF, the World Bank or the European Union, hold sway over aspects of the internal affairs of sovereign states. When those taking the decisions or contributing to policy formation are identified as Jewish, as for example during the unhappy tenure of Paul Wolfowitz at the World Bank or the Hollywood executives who shape part of global popular film culture, then that placing of someone thought to be powerful in a separate category of being a Jew is already the first step to antisemitic politics.

When Paine and Voltaire railed against their *anciens régimes*, they sought political freedoms. John Stuart Mill added a doctrine of freedom of expression and opinion: 'If all of mankind minus one, were of one opinion, and only one person were of the contrary opinion, mankind would be no more justified in silencing that one person, than he, if he had the power, would be justified in silencing mankind', with this qualification: 'The liberty of the individual must be thus far limited; he must not make himself a nuisance to other people.' This might be called the Wendell Holmes variation of absolute freedom of speech following the famous US chief justice who said there was no right to shout 'Fire!' in a crowded theatre. Blasphemous texts and images insulting God, Christ, Mohammed, Buddha or any of the differing prophets and divinities that religious believers worship or believe in are a matter of taste and decency. When Swiss Islamist ideologue Tariq Ramadan was linked to the successful Islamist campaign in Geneva on the anniversary of Voltaire's birth to stop a production of his play about Mohammed, he said it was a question of 'decency', not an act of censorship. Calling a campaign to ban a play a matter of politeness would have delighted Voltaire, who famously lived just across the border from the Swiss canton precisely to have a bolt-hole if the heavy hand of French absolutism moved against him.

Tariq Ramadan is the Swiss-born and educated grandson of Hasan al-Banna, the founder of the Muslim Brotherhood. He is charismatic, handsome, charming, fluent and a communicator without peer. In France, he attracts 'young Muslim women, with or without the veil, who sometimes travelled hundreds of kilometres to listen to him speak,' writes one of his biographers. As grandson of the founder of the Muslim Brotherhood, Ramadan has never made any secret of his relations with the Cairo-based Islamist organisation. His brother Hani runs the Geneva Islamic Centre and preaches a very strict Islam. *Le Monde* published an article by Hani Ramadan on 10 September 2002 in which he explained that stoning a woman to death for adultery was 'a punishment, but also a purification'.

Hasan al-Banna's ambitions for the movement were made clear in his *Epistle to Young People* written in the 1930s. Banna insisted that the Muslim Brotherhood refuses 'to recognise any organisation of government not based on Islamic foundations'. This Islamic government would replace all the states and nations stretching from Morocco to Yemen and taking in Syria and Egypt. Today's Islamists target all Arab states, especially those edging towards democracy and those willing to recognise Israel. Banna compared his Islamist political ambition to a contemporary European ideology: 'If the German

Reich insists it is the protector of all those with German blood in their veins, then the Muslim faith insists it can protect anyone who has learnt the Koran.'

It is of course unfair to visit the fundamentalist view of the grandfather on the grandson. One lived under the colonial occupation of Egypt and dealt with the corrupt rule of King Farouk, but it is pertinent to look at the conviction upon which the Brotherhood was established. From its foundation, the Muslim Brotherhood was a movement, not a membership organisation. Those who have studied its structures note its insistence on presenting a social face to local people while retaining an ideological hard core of belief and action. This allows the Brotherhood to distance itself when it chooses from violent action while still teaching and promoting an Islamist fundamentalism that allows no room for democracy, women's rights (in the 1930s the Brotherhood was writing to Cairo University demanding separate teaching for women and men students) or, above all, any space for Jews to live in peace in their own homeland. In 1948, Banna denounced 'World Jewry', who saw in the Muslim Brotherhood 'an important obstacle' to their ambitions. Above all, Hasan al-Banna glorified martyrdom and jihad, the highest stage of which he wrote 'is the armed struggle in the cause of God'. In 1946, Egypt's nationalist party, Wafd, denounced 'the fascist terror of the Muslim Brotherhood'.

Ramadan grew up in Geneva and has lived in the tolerant, liberal, open and democratic world of Europe. But Ramadan is a worrying figure despite his position. He spent some time as a schoolteacher in Geneva, and has been described by the *Washington Post* as the 'Martin Luther' of Islam, but unlike the German reformer the Geneva Islamist has shown no interest ever in challenging any of Islam's doctrine or practice. His writings are reverential. His book on Mohammed is described by the Islam scholar Malise Ruthven as 'a faith-promoting narrative, pleasant enough, but bland and colourless, that avoids any serious attempt to engage with traditional sources critically'. Ruthven, in particular, expressed concern that Ramadan glides over the cold-blooded murder of the men and women of a Jewish tribe, Banu Qurayzah, who refused Mohammed's dictatorship. Ramadan observes that this early murder of Jews ensured Mohammed's leadership: 'The fate meted out to the Banu Qurayzah men delivered a powerful message to all the neighbouring tribes that betrayals and aggressions would henceforth be severely punished.'

Is Ramadan a scholar, a preacher, a political activist or an ambassador in Europe for the theses of the Muslim Brotherhood founded by his grandfather? No one knows. Money has always been available to house him in different parts of Europe or pay for travel. The University of Geneva initially refused to award him a full doctorate when he first presented his thesis, which was seen as mainly an uncritical account of his grandfather's life and doctrine. He initiated action against the university. A second, more friendly committee was set up that accepted the thesis, which allows Ramadan the academic title of 'Dr'. He spent time in Cairo and studied in England, and gave a one-hour talk each week at the University of Fribourg in French-speaking Switzerland. He is often awarded the accolade of 'Professor' in the English-speaking media, but he has never held a chair, let alone a full-time teaching post at a university. His only full-time teaching post – the word for schoolteacher in French is *'professeur'*, which may explain the use of the title in English – was at a secondary school in Geneva, which he had to leave when he insisted on the need to teach creationism rather than the rationality of Darwin and scientific evolution. In an article for *Le Monde* published on

31 March 2005, he signed himself as 'Professor of Philosophy and Islamology at the University of Fribourg'. But when he was thus described, 'he was not a professor and had not taught at Fribourg for more than a year', writes one of his sympathetic biographers, the Swiss writer Ian Hamel. His charm and ability to deal politely and avoid giving offence to any non-Muslim audience he addresses make him difficult to pin down. He glides from country to country, from French to Arabic to English, operating in different nations' political-intellectual-media worlds that rarely interconnect.

Ramadan has stated: 'I accept laws as long as these laws do not oblige me to do something against my religion.' On the face of it what could be more reasonable? Ramadan continues: 'No declaration of human rights can make someone amputate themselves in order to become a (good) citizen . . . as some atheist, secular or Zionist ideologues insist.'

In a later book, *Islam, the West and the Challenges of Modernity*, Ramadan again refuses to accept the primacy of democracy over faith. He argues that Muslims come under two sources of authority.

> The first is that of the state which makes of each person a full-blooded citizen whereby there is no majority other than that resulting from the vote. The second is that of the religious community for which there exists an autonomy of worship, language and legislation (for personal affairs) . . . We can afford not to imitate the Western model of nation-state and still have the possibility of establishing other things.

In 2003, Ramadan outraged the French left when he wrote an article attacking a number of prominent French intellectuals and political activists. He described them as 'French Jewish intellectuals who previously could be considered as universal thinkers', but who now were simply supporters of Israel. Ramadan listed pell-mell left- and right-wing Jews and included one person, Pierre-André Taguieff, who has a Jewish-sounding name but is not a Jew. French socialists were astonished and upset at the antisemitic tone of Ramadan's remarks. The international analyst Alexandre Adler, who writes for the conservative *Figaro* paper, was lumped in with Bernard Kouchner, the former Socialist minister and founder of Médecins Sans Frontières who became France's foreign minister in 2007, and the independent *nouveau philosophe* writer Bernard-Henri Lévy. Identifying and attacking someone because they are Jewish was a speciality of the extreme right in France. For Ramadan to lose his self-control and lash out at intellectuals because they were Jews produced vivid, loud condemnations from the French left. Socialist Party leaders cut all contacts with him and Ramadan's status in France nose-dived.

At the time I was Europe minister in the British government. I was surprised that the Foreign Office under Jack Straw was considering inviting Ramadan to speak at a sensitive internal Foreign Office conference. No one consulted me even though I know France and – from many years living and working in Geneva, Ramadan's home city – I was aware of his contested record and reputation. The Muslim Council of Britain had one of its associates working in the Foreign Office, which was paying for Sheikh Qaradawi to attend FCO-sponsored conferences in Istanbul. By chance I was sharing a plane to a EU meeting when I noticed in amongst the papers in my red box the suggestion that the FCO should invite Ramadan to speak. I showed the then foreign secretary, Jack Straw, with whom I had serious differences on how to handle Islamist politics in Britain, an article in the independent left weekly, *Nouvel Observateur*. The article, which I happened to have in my briefcase, was critical of Ramadan's remarks on Jews. The FCO drew back from endorsing Ramadan after this outburst against Jewish intellectuals in France, but the Geneva activist popped up again as someone to be consulted by Whitehall, which rarely knows what is happening in the domestic politics of other countries.

After 9/11, Ramadan wrote an article in *Le Monde* that urged a 'total condemnation of the attacks in the United States', but then went on to ask: 'Who benefits from the attacks?' The answer, according to Ramadan, was the United States itself, which could now curtail civil liberty and launch a crusade against the Muslim world. The response, he argued, was for Muslims and non-Muslims to 'resist together' – not against the terrorism that slaughtered thousands in Manhattan, but against a United States seeking its riposte. Talking to young French Muslims in Lyon shortly after 9/11, Ramadan said there was no proof against Bin Laden and if there was a state that had an interest in committing the 9/11 murders it was Israel.

For Ramadan, killing Jewish children has to be understood in a context. Interviewed by the Italian news magazine *Panorama* in September 2004, at a moment when news pages reported on an 8-year-old Israeli child killed by suicide bombers, Ramadan said the act 'was morally condemnable but contextually understandable'. Ramadan will know the French phrase *'tout comprendre c'est tout pardonner'* ('to understand everything is to forgive everything'), so when he says that murdering a Jewish child in Israel is 'understandable', in whatever context, he enters the political world of justifying terror. In a debate with me at Oxford University in 2007, Ramadan agreed that Israel has a right to exist, which put him in a different place from many more fundamentalist Islamists. But he insisted on describing as 'resistance' the Jew-killers who enter Israel to end the lives of children or the aged. He sought, to my dismay, to make the comparison between the self-sacrifice of a soldier who died in the Second World War and the grooming of young people by older Islamists, who prepare their charges to blow themselves up with promises of meeting young women in paradise.

The Muslim Brotherhood is not a social-religious-political movement seeking power only through the ballot box or by peaceful persuasion. It has a history of violence. It organised the killing of Jews in Egypt in 1948 to persuade them to quit their homes. The same happened to Arabs in villages that Jews wanted to cleanse of Palestinians in 1948. Yet, do two wrongs make a right? The organisation tried to assassinate Nasser in 1954, and Muslim Brotherhood-inspired militants succeeded in murdering the Egyptian president, Anwar Sadat, in 1981. The latter's main crime in the eyes of Islamist ideologues was to have gone to the Knesset and dealt with Israel on a state-to-state basis. Ramadan uses the word 'execution', not 'murder', when dealing with the killing of Sadat. The brutality of Egyptian authorities against the Brotherhood, including the state killings of both Hasan al-Banna and Sayyid Qutb, the two main Muslim Brotherhood ideologues, cannot be excused. However, the refusal to condemn without equivocation or qualification appeals for 'understanding' of the murder of Jews in the region reduces Ramadan's status as a useful interlocutor.

That is why the principal and broad-front French anti-racist organisation SOS Racisme refused to have anything to do with Ramadan. The organisation came into being in the 1980s after police attacks on French black citizens demonstrating for their rights. The slogan *'Touche pas à mon pote'* ('Leave my mate alone'), with its symbol of an open hand rejecting the politics of difference, resonated around young

French people. Ramadan sought a meeting in Paris with the president of SOS Racisme, Malek Boutih. Boutih recalled later how Ramadan arrived in a hotel accompanied by burka-clad women and four bearded men to display his importance. But the two men quickly disagreed on the issue of the lay and secular norms of French republicanism. According to Boutih, there could be no question of Ramadan and his followers entering into an organisation that insisted on secularism as a key value in combating racism. For Boutih, Ramadan was speaking on behalf of the Muslim Brotherhood. Ramadan's rejection of core French republican values led the anti-racist leader to insult the Islamist: 'You are a fascist, no better than Jean-Marie Le Pen.' Even given the rhetorical extravagance of French political discourse, such a harsh insult was extraordinary. It is hard to explain in England or America the centrality of anti-religious thinking at the heart of French identity and republican citizenship. Even a devout Catholic like General de Gaulle refused to take communion when attending an official mass as president of France because he wanted to make clear his commitment to French politics and the French state being utterly separate from religion, faith and bishops. The arrival of Tariq Ramadan with his reverential approach to faith and his direct challenge to a system under which secular republican citizenship is recognised – not religious or racial identity – has made it difficult for him to make headway in France, despite his Francophone upbringing and the presence of Europe's biggest Muslim communities inside French borders.

In April 1998 in *Le Monde Diplomatique* Ramadan publicised the term 'Islamophobe' in an article praising the Runnymede Trust report, which put the phrase into circulation. Since then, Islamists in France have used the term as an insult against Muslim women who campaign against sexism and the violent abuse of women. The French women's rights organisation *Ni putes ni soumises* (Neither Whores Nor Submissive Women), which has fought for the application of universal human rights within France's female Muslim community, is regularly accused of 'Islamophobia', as Islamist misogynists have been given a stick to beat their female critics by the Runnymede Trust. The term is less used in France now, as even French left and third-world intellectuals have woken up to the difference between religion and ideology. They accept that to criticise the Islamist-sanctioned treatment of women and gays is not only permitted, but also a moral duty in a world in which women suffer so much at the hands of men asserting control in the name of religion. Speaking about gays, Ramadan stated: 'Homosexuality is not permitted in Islam and its public legalisation, as demanded in Europe, cannot be considered whether in terms of social recognition, as gay marriage nor in any other fashion.'

In 2002, Ramadan wrote the preface to that year's edition of fatwas issued by the European Council of Fatwas. The council president is Sheikh Qaradawi, whose fatwas have justified suicide bombing. When the council met in Stockholm in July 2003 it pronounced itself in favour of killing innocent Jewish civilians in Israel by means of suicide bombers. Yet Ramadan, quick to adjust to a different audience, was swift to condemn the 7/7 suicide bombing attacks on the London Underground, just as the Muslim Council of Britain issued a press release after the failed terror attacks at Glasgow airport and in London two years later.

Tariq and his brother Hani were also open supporters of the Islamist movement in Algeria, which organised a violent uprising after the secular and military state annulled elections in 1990. Many of the Muslim Brotherhood preachers and organisers harassed and expelled by the Egyptian authorities crossed into Algeria to encourage the implantation of Islamism in the oil- and gas-rich but corrupt and authoritarian one-party state. Under pressure from Europe, the Maghreb countries (Morocco, Tunisia and Algeria) sought to increase democratic participation. But they flinched from handing power to the totalising Islamist politics that rose as the only alternative. The example of Iran, where the authoritarianism of the Shah was replaced by the far worse cruelty, torture, executions and repressions of religious rule, was a model not to be imitated. Alain Gresh is editor of *Le Monde Diplomatique*. He promotes Islamism and Ramadan in his illiberal, anti-Occidental monthly. Once he introduced Ramadan to an audience with the observation that: 'The peril of Islamism is an echo of the peril of communism which we have heard about over fifty years.' But the communist peril so casually dismissed by the Paris intellectual was real enough to the Poles, Czechs, Hungarians and others who had their freedoms denied and their lives limited by living under a totalising 'ism'.

Is Ramadan seeking to modernise Islam or Islamise modernity? The jury is out. Seven biographies have already been published in French. The Geneva-educated Ramadan has French as his first language. Most of his more controversial activities, such as his involvement in preventing the production in Geneva in 1993 of Voltaire's play on Mohammed as well as his anti-Jewish remarks in connection with the meeting in Paris in 2003 of the European Social Forum, have taken place in the Francophone world. His refusal in a widely watched television debate in France to call for the abolition of the practice sanctioned by sharia law of stoning women to death shocked many who had been his admirers.

Ramadan likes to cites the example of the Justice and Development Party that rules Turkey. It undoubtedly originates in political Islamism. It has won power democratically in Turkey and insists it wants to take Turkey in the direction of European Union membership. However, it has came to power after eighty years of Kemalist rule in Turkey and the enforced secularisation of society. Kemal Atatürk swept away the archaic Muslim rules that had imprisoned Turkish women in a backward-looking world hostile to any aspect of early twentieth-century modernity. He made films of himself dancing in order to show that men and women could be together in public. He stationed police officers on crossroads to sweep off the tarbush or fez, the Tommy Cooper-style head-gear that Muslim men wore under the Caliphate. He did not seek to abolish religion, as happened further north in Lenin's Russia, but he was clear that Turkey would never grow if constrained by Muslim political rule.

Today's rulers of Turkey appear to have accepted that faith is a private matter. Ankara has good relations with Tel Aviv. Like the post-war Christian Democrats who arose in Europe in place of clericalist right-wing Catholic parties, the Turkish experiment in Islamic democracy is important. Other countries with majority Muslim populations like Indonesia or Malaysia, or like India with its 200 million-strong Muslim minority population, can manage to hold democratic elections, have a free press and allow other freedoms that no Arab Muslim state or Iran enjoys. The Turkish example is indeed important. It starts, however, from a rejection of nearly all the Islamist precepts Ramadan has supported during his career. Muslim Brotherhood writing denounced Kemalism as a major foe that Islamism had to defeat. Hasan al-Banna wanted to reverse the abolition of the Caliphate; the restoration of Caliphate rule is a demand of many Islamist groups today. That it won't happen is irrelevant. Few of the young Muslim citizens in Europe drawn into the politics of restoring the Caliphate know the history of Turkey or the invocations of Hitler and Mussolini made by the Islamists before the 1940s. It is the power of the simple message, the vision of Utopian Islamic rule, that seduces. The task of the honest intellectual active in politics is gently – sometimes brutally – to disillusion believers in myths.

Tariq Ramadan continues to hide behind anti-Zionism. As François Garaï, a liberal rabbi in Geneva who has often spoken with Ramadan, says: 'He is not fundamentally antisemitic. But he is fundamentally antizionist . . . and sometimes antizionism glides into antisemitism.' Unless and until Ramadan is explicit in rejecting all murders, political violence and the tactics of terror that lead old men to send children to kill, it will be hard for him to avoid the charge of double standards. Ramadan could choose to be a John Hume, a proud Catholic nationalist appalled by the suffering of his community and co-religionists at the hands of Protestant supremacist bigots in Ulster, but nonetheless outright in his condemnation of terrorist violence that the IRA and Sinn Fein dressed up as 'resistance'. He could be inspired by or seek to emulate the example of a Gandhi, a Mandela, a Sakharov, a Havel or a Wei Jingsheng, all of whom resisted oppression non-violently. Instead, Ramadan uses part of the vocabulary of those willing to kill Jews in order to hurt Israel, while simultaneously presenting himself as a guide for European Muslims seeking to be at home in modern Europe. Until, however, the ultimate expression of antisemitism – the murder of Jews for political reason – is expunged from the thought, word and deed of those calling for peace, human rights and respect for Palestinian identity, the chances of changing the politics of the region are slim and Europe's Muslim population will fail to have a leadership based on truth speaking to the power of Islamist ideology.

8

Conspiracies, Cabals and the 'Lobby'

Antisemitism is like a store of energy. It will never entirely disappear, but it can increase in size and strength. The object of democratic politics should be to minimise this reservoir. The unwitting effect of much of the discussion about Jews is to feed dislike of them and their causes. The most enduring of all the antisemitic tropes is that of the Jewish lobby – the cabal, the Jews in high places, the Jews controlling decision-making at all levels of power. *Corriere della Serra*, Italy's leading newspaper, carried a front-page comment in August 2007. Under the heading 'The Eternal Scapegoat', the paper reprimanded a well-known priest, Don Gelmini, who had been named in reports in connection with alleged paedophile inquiries. Don Gelmini said the accusations had been got up by a 'Jewish radical-chic lobby'. The priest clearly thought that invoking the word 'lobby' and linking it to Jews would deflect his accusers, winning support for his position. Across Europe the term 'lobby' is becoming a new scattergun device for accusing Jews anywhere of exercising secret and sinister power.

This central aim, to present Jews as a people apart, takes many shapes. Former French premier Raymond Barre, a right-wing economist who translated Milton Friedman into French before becoming French prime minister in 1976, won notoriety in 1980 when an antisemitic bomb attack killed four people near a synagogue in Paris. As prime minister, he deplored the bomb attack because it 'was aimed at Jews going to the Synagogue and hit innocent French people'. The proposition that those murdered in this antisemitic atrocity – all French citizens – should be divided up into those who were Jewish and those who were French came as a shock to many in France. Memories are still raw among those who remember how the Paris police divided Parisians into Jewish and non-Jewish groups, and handed the former over to the Germans for deportation to death camps. After leaving office Raymond Barre became mayor of Lyon and a speaker on the circuit of conservative politics in France. In the French presidential election of 2007, a few months before he died, he referred to the Jewish 'lobby' as having too much power in France.

Barre used the English word 'lobby' because he knew that bringing in a foreign word to describe something he sought to denounce would add an esoteric flavour to his old-fashioned French conservative antisemitism. The term 'lobby' is now a codeword used by open and unwitting antisemites as they dip into the rattlebag of old antisemitic terminology and seek to update it. Just as the word 'cabal' comes from the initials of the names of five Privy Councillors who formed the proto-government under Charles II in the seventeenth century, so too the word 'lobby' has harmless and precise roots in English parliamentary terminology. But just as references to a Jewish 'cabal' came to be used by old antisemites, so today's antisemites have fastened on the Jewish, 'Kosher' (to use the *New Statesman* headline) or Israel 'lobby' to punt the line that Jews exert improper influence.

Lobbies are central to all democratic politics. Every day as an MP I receive requests, and sometimes more strident demands, that I support or endorse this or that cause. It is an integral part of democratic politics and is even reflected in the names to areas in the Houses of Parliament. Every British citizen is entitled to enter the Central Lobby. I once had an American intern working for me in the Commons and when I took him on his first guided tour, he looked in awe at the teeming Central Lobby as crowds milled around, telling their MPs how to vote. He had worked on Capitol Hill in Washington and asked me amazed: 'You let your voters get this close?!' Well, yes we do. British democracy is based on an eternal clash of lobbies. Party politics is based around the great enduring lobbies or interests of land, the aristocracy and right-wing causes for the Conservatives, and social justice, minority rights and enhanced collective provision in areas like health and education for Labour.

So the lobby is the place where men and women, power and influence, meet and discuss matters of public interest in privacy. It has gone into more general usage to mean a pressure group, for example the human rights lobby, the Catholic lobby, the agricultural lobby or just about anyone who wants to call up a politician to ask for support. The implicit (understood, if unspoken) threat is that if the politician does not offer support, then whoever is doing the lobbying will not offer support for that politician's re-election.

Every student of British history knows the power of lobbies in America. The hand of Britain was stayed in terms of its treatment of Ireland after the First World War because of the clamour of the Irish lobby in the United States. More darkly, in the 1970s and 1980s the Irish lobby in the United States contributed to the murder of innocent British children, women and civilian men as American money was pumped into the hands of the terrorist IRA. As a supporter of Turkey's modernisation and someone who has worked to try and persuade Turkey to think of a European rather than a Middle East destiny I have met in Congress with fellow politicians who think similarly on Turkey. One of my oldest political friends worked as a lobbyist for the Greek Cypriot community, trying to uphold the rights of the sovereign republic of Cyprus after it was invaded and occupied by the Turkish military in 1974. And no doubt European workers and their trade unions recall the lobbying power of the American unions who insisted to successive administrations that free independent and democratic trade unions should be part of the reconstruction of Europe after 1945.

There is nothing new in the fact of an effective Jewish lobby in the United States. What is different, however, is the claim made by two American professors that there is a far-reaching network of Jews in the United States, which they call 'The Israel Lobby'. As the Hollywood actor Mel Gibson so charmingly put it, 'The Jews are responsible for all the wars in the world.' Well-known preacher Billy Graham also believed in secret Jewish influences in America, telling his friend President Nixon in 1972 that Jews had a 'stranglehold' on the American media. Graham declared that 'the Jewish stranglehold has got to be broken or the country's going down the drain'. Graham later apologised for his remarks and said he remained a supporter of Israel. The Reverend Graham was not the first, nor the last antisemitic supporter of Israel. Three decades later two academics have written hundreds of pages to make essentially the same point as the Reverend Graham. The two professors, John J. Mearsheimer and Stephen M. Walt, are at the end of their careers as university-based academics who specialise in foreign policy. Both belong loosely to what is called the realist school of foreign policy analysts. The supreme pontiff of this school, of course, is Henry Kissinger, whose hero was the Austrian, Prince

Metternich. Realists want stability and see only national interests to be defended, not universal values to be promoted. That deep yearning to avoid foreign entanglements, as George Washington called them, is part of America's foreign policy gene pool. But for the two professors such discussion of the complexities of how foreign policy decisions are arrived at is too messy and contradictory. How much easier it is to shape a thesis that attributes what the United States does in the Middle East to a principal source of influence – the Jews.

Over a quarter of a century of regularly visiting the United States and taking part in seminars and discussions on different aspects of international politics, as well as devouring all the books on policy that Dupont Circle has to offer, I must have read a hundred articles, papers and references to the Israel lobby. Why then did these two professors find themselves catapulted to fame as if like a Newton or Einstein they had discovered something that no one else had noticed or defined previously? Despite being occupants of the rarefied world of the academic monograph and the review article in serious academic journals, they started to pen a piece for the *Atlantic Monthly*, the US editorial magazine on politics and foreign affairs. Their basis, as they explain in their book *The Israel Lobby and U.S. Foreign Policy*, was to discuss those very subjects. Their article took three years to write, and in 2005 the editor of the *Atlantic Monthly* decided not to run it. Instead it was sent to the *London Review of Books* and to the surprise of no one who reads that journal, with its constant prejudice against Israel and the US, the article was published, accompanied by carefully constructed propaganda claiming it had been censored or suppressed in the United States.

It is unclear why the two professors, who have plenty of access to other outlets in America, chose not to publish their paper in an American journal. It contained nothing new beyond the well-known examples of Jewish groups seeking to influence how policy-makers in the United States come to their decisions on Israel. The article and the book made allegations that American Jews decided US foreign policy on Iran, Iraq and Syria, and both the article and the subsequent book were entirely solipsistic. There is not a single reference to any of the European policy discussions on the Middle East or a book published in a European language.

There is some discussion of Europe itself, but only to make the bizarre claim that European antisemitism 'was actually declining'. They quote one poll of French citizens in 2002, which claimed amongst other things that 'eighty-five per cent of practicing French Catholics rejected the charge that Jews have too much influence on business and finance'. At times, their approach to antisemitism seems to border on a denial of its existence. This, for example, is how they describe one of the post-war world's most notorious Jew-hating antisemites: 'Sayyid Qutb, the Egyptian *dissident* [my emphasis] whose writings have been an important inspiration for contemporary Islamic fundamentalists.'

Reading Qutb's antisemitic and anti-democracy tracts is a reminder of what faces democracy as it confronts the new ideology of antisemitism. In August 2007, the Foreign Affairs Select Committee of the House of Commons published a report on the Middle East. Its headline recommendation was that talks should take place with Hamas, the name of the Islamic Resistance Movement, which is powerful amongst many Palestinians. Hamas, of course, has links to the Muslim Brotherhood, and thus to Qutb, whom Mearsheimer and Walt describe as a dissident. So a reading of the Hamas Charter adopted in 1988 is useful. It is one of the most antisemitic, Jew-hating political statements ever published in history.

For Hamas, 'Our struggle against the Jews is extremely wide-ranging and grave, so much so that it will need all the loyal efforts we can wield, to be followed by further steps and reinforced by successive battalions from the multifarious Arab and Islamic world, until the enemies are defeated'. Thus, in the very first lines of the Charter, Hamas adherents are told: 'Israel will rise and will remain erect until Islam eliminates it.'

The Charter quotes the Prophet Mohammed: 'Muslims will fight the Jews (and kill them); until the Jews hide behind rocks and trees, which will cry O Muslim! There is a Jew hiding behind the tree, come on and kill him!' One might be tempted to dismiss these invocations to kill Jews as simply religious fundamentalist language from the Koran, not to be taken literally. But the Hamas Charter rather contradicts the well-meaning wishes of British MPs by rejecting the idea that talking with their opponents is fruitful. On the contrary, Hamas declares, 'the so-called peaceful solutions, and the international conferences to resolve the Palestinian problem, are all contrary to the beliefs of [Hamas] . . . these conferences are no more than a means to appoint the non-believers as arbitrators in the lands of Islam.'

So much for the hopes of a reconciliation between Hamas and the more secular wing of the Palestinian movement, Fatah. Indeed, in Article 27 of the Charter, Hamas makes clear that 'despite the fact that we do not denigrate [the PLO's] role in the Arab-Israeli conflict, we cannot substitute it for the Islamic nature of Palestine by adopting secular thought'. For Hamas, 'there is no solution to the Palestinian problem except by Jihad. The initiatives, proposals and international conferences are a waste of time, an exercise in futility.' Instead, Hamas 'must imprint on the minds of generations of Muslims that the Palestinian problem is a religious one, to be dealt with on this premise.' Talking with Hamas may well be necessary but those advocating such a policy cannot dismiss the core contempt of the Hamas Constitutional Charter not just for Jews but for fellow Palestinians who are secular rather than Islamist.

So, with the PLO, secular politics and the idea of peace conferences all dismissed, Hamas turns to its real enemy – the Jew. 'The Nazism of the Jews . . . scares everyone. They make war against people's livelihood, plunder their moneys and threaten their honour.' For Hamas, the Jews are the immortal enemy with huge power to influence world history, past and present. Jewish money is used 'to take over control of the world media such as news agencies, the press, publication houses, broadcasting and the like'. This vision of Jews controlling the media links up with the British National Party's view, expressed in Nick Griffin's publication, *Who Are the Mindbenders*, that Jews, open or those who have changed their names in order to hide their Jewishness, are in control of the media in Britain.

Hamas goes further. The Jews 'stood behind the French and Communist revolutions and behind most of the revolutions we hear about'. This may come as news to biographers of Danton and Robespierre, as well as Lenin and the anti-semitic Stalin. More recent revolutionary movements like, say, Castro's takeover in Cuba or the Chinese Communist capture of power, do not seem especially linked to Jews. Yet Hamas tells its followers that Jews

established the League of Nations in order to rule the world. The Jews stood behind World War 2, where they collected immense benefits from trading with war materials . . . They inspired the establishment of the United Nations and the Security Council to replace the League of Nations, in order to

130

rule the world by their intermediary. There was no war that broke anywhere without their fingerprints on it.

Article 22 of the Charter also reveals the names of further enemies of Muslims. The Jews use 'money to establish clandestine organisations which are spreading around the world, in order to destroy societies and carry out Zionist interests. Such organisations are: the Freemasons, Rotary Clubs, Lions Clubs . . . All of them are nests of saboteurs and sabotage.' In three separate articles of the Charter, Hamas denounces the Rotary Club and similar outfits, which 'act for the interests of Zionism . . . to wipe out Islam'. So the next time your local Rotary rattles a can to raise money for charity, remember the warning from Hamas that the Masons, Rotary and the Lions are all secret Zionist organisations dedicated to do down Islam.

Perhaps realising that anyone who took the trouble to read the Hamas Charter would find its language repulsive, Jew-hating and as unacceptable as anything in the long history of antisemitism, Article 31 tries to soften the line by declaring,

> Hamas is a humane movement, which cares for human rights and is committed to tolerance . . . Under the shadow of Islam it is possible for the members of the three religions: Islam, Christianity and Judaism to coexist in safety and security . . . [But] the members of the other religions must desist from struggling against Islam over sovereignty in the region.

Having made that generous offer the Hamas Charter reverts to the language of 'Nazi Zionist practices', just in case any reader was beginning to think a chink of normal humanity might be emerging, and the very next article, 32, goes on to make clear that in the view of Hamas, 'Zionist scheming has no end, and after Palestine they will covet expansion from the Nile to the Euphrates . . . Their scheme has been laid out in *The Protocols of the Elders of Zion*.'

Today's politicians and diplomatists may dismiss the language of the Hamas Charter as just extravagant, excited and excessive words from Islamists who can be cajoled and coaxed into the compromises necessary for the establishment of a Palestinian state alongside Israel. That may be so, and it is clearly desirable. Yet the Hamas Charter stands as one of the most virulent expressions of Jew-hatred ever written down. It was written not in 1888, but in 1988, and it still stands today.

Ten years later, in 1998, Mohammad Riad, a Hezbollah MP and member of its political council, explained to the writer Amal Saad-Ghorayeb why killing Jewish children was part of Hezbollah's project: 'We know that the emotions and sympathy that are associated with [the killing of] children differ from those associated with adults . . . This child may have been killed but it is the project that brought him [to Israel] that is responsible for his oppression, not the person who killed him.' Hezbollah exists as an Islamist organisation in Lebanon and since the Israeli withdrawal from southern Lebanon it might be assumed that the struggle was over. Not so. The desire to kill Jews remains overwhelming. According to Riad, Jews connived with the Nazis on the Holocaust: 'From what we know about the Jews, their tricks and their deception, we do not think it unlikely that they partook in the planning of the Holocaust. [They] prepared the foreground which incited the Nazis to the Holocaust killings, so that they could serve their settlement project in Palestine.'

Hezbollah's deputy leader is Naim Qasim. He does not bother with any of the usual double-talk that he and his movement oppose Zionism but are not antisemitic. 'The history of the Jews has proven that, regardless of the Zionist proposal, they are a people who are evil in their ideas,' Qasim declares. As the chronicler of Hezbollah, Amal Saad-Ghorayeb argues 'the party insists that its strong aversion to Judaism is unrelated to its abomination of Zionism and hence exists irrespective of the existence of Zionism'.

Hezbollah looks to Iran and to Shi'ite, rather than Sunni Islamist writings like those of Qutb, for inspiration. Qutb's centrality to twenty-first-century Islamism is not in dispute. So it jars when Mearsheimer and Walt use the noble term 'dissident' to describe Sayyid Qutb. This is to place one of the twentieth century's worst Jew-haters on the same plane as a Sakharov or a Havel. They do go on to note that Qutb was 'hostile to the United States both because he saw it as a corrupt and licentious society and also because of US support for Israel'. Qutb's principal antisemitic and anti-Western tracts were written in the early 1950s before the United States had become a fully fledged supporter of Israel. To award a roaring antisemite – who would not have been outdone by Himmler or Streicher – the title of a 'dissident' who was an 'inspiration' is, to put it politely, a curious judgement.

Mearsheimer and Walt go on to argue 'there is in fact abundant evidence that US support for Israel encourages anti-Americanism throughout the Arab and Islamic world and has fuelled the rage of anti-American terrorists'. It would be more accurate for the two authors to write not of the rage of anti-American terrorists, but of anti-Western, anti-European or anti-democratic terrorists. But the moment they lift their eyes beyond the horizon of the United States their thesis dissolves. Loud and active as Jewish groups are in defence of Israel in some European countries, they are massively outnumbered in Europe by Muslim French, British, Spanish or German citizens, exercising their democratic rights as voters or as activists in party politics. What Mearsheimer and Walt are not willing to accept is that the action of terrorist organisations under the banner of Islamist fundamentalism is action aimed specifically at Jews, secondly at the Jewish state of Israel and thirdly at all democratic values – though not necessarily in that order. America woke up after 9/11 and realised it was not immune from the rage of the new criminal ideology that confronts the twenty-first-century democratic world.

Mearsheimer and Walt claim to have revealed that the lobby is responsible for the difficulties that the United States has with Iran. This falsely builds up the power of Jews in America in a way that makes little sense to a European. Every European leader from President Putin to President Sarkozy, speaking to the United Nations in September 2007, has said that Iran's steady march to becoming a nuclear armed state is unacceptable. The two professors do not mention Iran's state sponsorship for antisemitism. The threat of the president of Iran to wipe Israel off the map of the world or his sponsorship for the first exhibition since 1945 of anti-semitic 'art' get no discussion. Instead Mearsheimer and Walt say that the statements by Ahmadinejad 'are more accurately seen as tactical measures intended to improve Iran's overall position in the region'. There were many who thought that Hitler's remarks about Jews before 1933 should be discounted and were clever Nazi tactics to win power in Germany.

I shared the hopes of the then British foreign secretary Jack Straw as he worked with Germany's foreign minister, Joschka Fischer, on Iran. Fischer has a great sensitivity to the Middle East and devoted much of his time as Europe's senior foreign minister to trying to find solutions to the region's problems. Married to an Iranian, he is deeply sensitive to the difficulties of his wife's country. Straw even extended to a televised press conference in Tehran in which he referred to the Prophet Mohammed, adding 'peace be upon his name'. It was odd to hear a British foreign minister use a Muslim trope in a nation that certainly would not offer the same respect from the mouth of its chief foreign policy spokesman then or now to the Catholic or other faiths. Straw had genuinely striven in his own constituency to integrate and to help the Muslim immigrants from both Pakistan and India who together with their families form a sizeable part of his electorate. But to little avail in Iran, where the Iranian regime showed nothing but contempt for well-meaning European efforts to find a diplomatic resolution to its determined Shia ideological expansionism (based on a fundamental hatred of Jews and Israel) and relentless march towards full nuclear weapon status.

I have argued in *Newsweek* and many European publications for the full diplomatic recognition of Iran by the United States. But unlike Mearsheimer and Walt, I have few illusions that simply being nice to Iran can deflect the Jew- and Israel-hating Iranian regime from sparking a new, regional nuclear arms race. Sunni states will not stand idly by as an expansionist Shia ideology becomes a nuclear power. For the two professors, however, the worries of the Sunni states in every Muslim country that confronts jihadi fundamentalism will come as a surprise.

But before we go further, it is worth seeing where those who think it is Jews who determine US policy come from. In a revealing interview with *The Nation*, Professor Mearsheimer said that until recently his knowledge of Israel was limited . He said he 'had been blinded' by the Leon Uris novel *Exodus*. This book and the subsequent film were highly romanticised versions of the birth of Israel. It is hard to believe that a serious American foreign policy academic had read nothing of the historical work on the early years of Israel, which showed a much clearer picture of ruthless ethnic cleansing of Arabs and military land grabs facilitated by the foolish decision of Arab states to invade Israel after the UN had permitted the creation of the Jewish state. Indeed, as early as 1948 the director of the Israeli Labour Party's Arab Department said that 'the robbery, killing, expulsion and rape of the Arabs could reach such proportions that we would no longer be able to stand'.

Those who welcomed the article when it appeared in the *London Review of Books* claimed that it was impossible to be published in the United States if the writer was critical of Israel. Yet one of the most prestigious and serious of American publishing houses, Farrar, Straus and Giroux, paid a reported $350,000 advance to Mearsheimer and Walt for the book-length version of their argument after seeing the interest stirred up by the controversy. Far from the Jewish lobby stopping critical discussion of Israel in the United States, it would appear that writing a book on the power and influence of the lobby is the quickest way to make serious money as an American academic.

There continues to be much debate and argument about the role of Jews in influencing US policy, and not all agree with Mearsheimer and Walt. Noam Chomsky argued that the two authors had ignored the deeper forces in the American economy that wanted a war with Iraq. Alan Greenspan argues in his memoirs that protecting US supplies of oil was the main cause of the war. And try as they might to highlight people with Jewish names, like Paul Wolfowitz, who were players in American foreign policy-making circles after 2000, the uncomfortable fact for their thesis is that President George W. Bush, Vice President Dick Cheney, Secretary of

State Colin Powell, National Security Advisor Condoleezza Rice, the American Chiefs of Staff, the rumbustious UN Ambassador John Bolton, Defense Secretary Donald Rumsfeld and others who argued for a tough line against Iraq and any other state linked to terrorism were all Christian or non-religious figures whose connection to Jews was limited. President George W. Bush himself came from a patrician East Coast family, who probably went to schools and had member-ship of clubs to which few if any Jews were admitted. For Mearsheimer and Walt, however, it is the Israel lobby that is responsible for US policy in the Middle East. Their article and book was seized on by every Jew-hater and anti-American around the world. Guilt by association is intellectually and morally unacceptable, but if I were to write a book that was seized on by people I loathed and detested, and opposed personally and politically, as proof that one of their core theses was right and justified, perhaps I might pause and reflect a moment. There is no such self-awareness on offer from the good professors.

This is not the place to enter into a debate about the inter-vention in Iraq in 2003. History may decide that it would have been better to leave Saddam in place, to contain rather than confront him and ignore the manifest failure of the UN to enforce its own resolution and leave Saddam supporting the global jihad against democracy. All I can report is that Jews, Israel and the fabled 'lobby' did not exist in any papers I saw or discussions I had as a government minister. What did strike me was the emergence of a neutralist-pacifist hostility to the US at the highest level of Germany. It was a first in post-war Europe. The French, instead of grandstanding with rhetoric at the UN, would have done well to make clear from the beginning that they would never take part in military action against Saddam. I wish I could believe that the UK and its friends and allies would never again be paralysed over whether or not to take action against a tyrant who defies the UN, has a proven record of invading other countries, sponsoring and validating terrorism outside his borders, and who inflicts cruelty and mass murder on his people without a second's thought. Foreign policy success has many fathers; Iraq is an orphan. But what is important is to learn the lessons of the strategic and tactical errors made in the run-up to March 2003 and the occupation that followed.

This whole policy debate will only be deformed, however, if the smears against Jews from academics like Mearsheimer and Walt are allowed to stand. Their book was swiftly translated and became a best-seller on all the Israel- and Jew-hating bookstalls of the world. They have $350,000 in their bank accounts, but the cause of peace and the defeat of terror and tyranny is weakened by men like this.

It is also weakened by political leaders who deny the threat we face. In his powerful book *Celsius 7/7*, the British Conservative MP and Shadow Cabinet member Michael Gove castigates intellectuals of the left and right who

argue that, given the general level of Muslim discontent, we should abandon intervention altogether, so as not to antagonise Islamic opinion. It is worthwhile to ask whether it would ever be right for a democracy to give veto power over its foreign policy to any particular minority, but it is particularly worthwhile to reflect on the wisdom of allowing a specific religious minority's sensibilities to dictate a country's relations with the rest of the world.

Mr Gove is right. Which is why it is disappointing to read his party leader's attack on the policy of intervening against tyranny, torture and terror in a defining foreign policy speech in Berlin in October 2007.

Mr Cameron has also repudiated the use of the political term 'Islamist' in connection with crimes carried out by those claiming to be inspired by Islamist texts and appeals. More recently, the Conservative Party's Muslim Group has produced policy recommendations criticising British foreign policy on Israel and urging an avoidance of acts that might offend Islamist politics across the world. No action is taken to repudiate this group or dismiss its chairman, who sits for the Conservatives in the House of Lords. David Cameron is a possible future British prime minister, and were this to happen he would join that elite group known as leaders of the free world. Will he buy into the Mearsheimer and Walt thesis about a Jewish lobby dictating Middle East policy? Or will Mr Gove's more robust language win the day? Time will tell.

9

Antisemitism and Israel

Some years ago at Rotherham market in South Yorkshire I bought about thirty old volumes of *Encyclopaedia Britannica* dating from the beginning of the last century and before. The tenth edition of *Encyclopaedia Britannica* was published in 1902 and has a long section on antisemitism. The ninth edition, published a quarter of a century earlier, had no such entry. Jew-hatred had been around for two millennia, but antisemitism as a politics, a movement, as über-nationalism, as racism suddenly erupted into existence in the short space of the quarter-century separating the two editions of *Encyclopaedia Britannica*: nothing on antisemitism in 1875, but by the beginning of the twentieth century it was impossible to ignore the new phenomenon. In the 1902 edition, a learned twelve-page entry was written by Lucien Wolf, president of the Jewish Historical Society of England. Antisemitism filled the space between Antioch and Antitoxin. There are detailed descriptions of antisemitism in Russia, France, Germany and Romania, with its English expression finding place in the hostility to the arrival of the Jewish Benjamin Disraeli as prime minister. A biography of Disraeli quoted in the *Encyclopedia Britannica* entry 'pictured him as the instrument of the Jewish people, "moulding the whole policy of Christendom to Jewish aims"'.

The author insisted that: 'Antisemitism is exclusively a

question of European politics, and its origin is to be found, not in the long struggle between Europe and Asia, or between the Church and the Synagogue, which filled so much of ancient and medieval history, but in the social conditions resulting from the emancipation of the Jews in the middle of the nineteenth century.' Modern sociology and class politics had now arrived and readers were informed:

> The Jews, however, through no fault of their own, belonged to the industrial bourgeoisie. Into that class all the strength was thrown, and owing to their ghetto preparation, they rapidly took a leading place in it, politically and socially. When the mid-century revolutions made the bourgeoisie the ruling power in Europe, the *semblance* [my emphasis] of a Hebrew domination presented itself.

Wolf finishes his survey optimistically:

> Antisemitism has . . . left no permanent mark on the social and political evolution of Europe. Its racial doctrine is at best a crude hypothesis; its nationalist theory has only served to throw into striking relief the essentially economic basis of modern society, while its political activity has revealed the vulgarity and ignorance which constitutes its main source of strength.

The supreme self-confidence of English imperial liberalism in its final glory years of Edward VII rings out. On the contrary, argues the author, 'So far from injuring the Jews . . . [antisemitism] has given a new spirit and a new source of strength to Judaism', which he identified as 'the so-called Zionist movement' combined with efforts 'to unite the Jewish people in an effort to raise the Jewish character and to promote a higher consciousness of the dignity of the race'. Evidence of this arose from the fact that 'in the whole history of Judaism, perhaps, there have been no more numerous or remarkable instances of reversions to the faith than during the last thirty years'. Inadvertently, he highlighted a truth which twenty-first-century antisemites might ponder. The more the Jews are persecuted or driven into a corner, the more they discover inner strengths and invent a new sense of identity and self-awareness, of which the Zionist movement, the offspring of late nineteenth-century antisemitism, is one example.

The *Encyclopaedia Britannica* author writing in 1902 was cautiously confident but aware of dangers ahead. Antisemitism

has been unmasked and discredited, [but] it is to be feared that its history is not yet at an end. While there are in Russia and Rumania six million of Jews who are being systematically degraded, and who periodically overflow the western frontier, there will continue to be a Jewish question in Europe; and while there are weak Governments, as in Austria and France, and ignorant and superstitious elements in the enfranchised classes of those countries, that question will seek to play a part in politics.

A century later, we can see how right he was to be prudent. Yet still the fascinating question tugs at our sleeves. If antisemitism didn't exist, would Israel exist in its present form?

The search to have one tiny corner of the planet where Jews might live on their own terms was a direct response to the organised antisemitism of the late nineteenth and much of the twentieth century. The Zionist dream of Jews returning to the land of their book and prophets has, of course, held good for more than 2,000 years. But the modern political movement of Zionism aimed at creating a nation-state where Jews would not be persecuted started in Europe 120 years ago in response to the transformation of antisemitism into political ideology. To read the antisemitic texts of nineteenth-century intellectuals in France and Germany, who subtly metamorphosed antisemitism into serious politics, is to be not only shocked, but also in awe that so few people could produce so much hate. The pogroms of the Russian empire that then covered many of the proud nations of eastern and south-eastern Europe made Jews look for somewhere, anywhere, that offered a home. In 1900 there were about fifty identifiable nation-states in the world; now there are nearly 200. In 1990 there was one Yugoslavia; now seven nations, partly impelled by Catholic, Muslim and Orthodox religious affiliation, exist on what was once Yugoslav territory. And as Flemish, Scottish, Catalan, Kurdish, Welsh, Québécois, Koso-van, Ossetian, Tibetan, Tamil and other claims for nation-state status grow the twenty-first century will see scores of new countries coming into being.

One of those – and the sooner, the better – will be a functioning Palestinian state. The tragedy of the Palestinians is not the existence of Israel, but the failure to create their own state. The British journalist Bill Deedes reported in 1937 that a British government commission, the Peel Commission, called for 'separate sovereign states for Jews and Arabs'. The proposal was rejected by Palestinian leaders under the sway of the Nazi-sympathising Grand Mufti of Jerusalem, Haj Amin al-Husseini, the uncle of Yasser Arafat. Between 1948 and 1967 Jordan and Egypt occupied and placed under the sovereignty of Cairo and Amman the territory that might have composed a Palestinian state. No one talked of 'occupation' in that era. For many in the West who opine or are militant on Israel and Palestinian rights, history began in 1967. Had Nasser and allied Arab states stayed their military hand and sought some modus vivendi with Israel after it became clear in 1948 and again in 1956 that Israeli military power would not be defeated, then Jerusalem today would still be a divided city.

Writing on Gaza, Perry Anderson argues that 'the EU showed no more hesitation than the US in plunging the population into misery, cutting off all aid when voters elected the wrong government, on the pretext that it must first recognise the Israeli state, as if Israel had ever recognised a Palestinian state'. Two points are worth making. First, Hamas could, indeed, try to challenge the Israel/US/EU line, as defined by Anderson, by stating the obvious that Israel exists and has a right to exist. Second, why is it Israel's fault that no state of Palestine was created on the territories (minus Israel as sanctioned by the UN in 1947–8) that were historically Palestinian? A question that Egyptian, Jordanian, Lebanese and Syrian historians might address one day. After the 2006 Lebanon conflict, Hezbollah gave $12,000 to every person who was left homeless as a result of the fighting. Just imagine if the leaders of the oil-rich Arab countries after 1948, or indeed states like Egypt, Syria or Jordan, had offered similar generous terms to those displaced and expelled from their homes when the Arab states decided to try and snuff out the existence of Israel after the UN gave birth to the Jewish state. After 1945, West Germany absorbed twelve million people expelled from territories that for centuries had been German. It would have been possible to create a Palestinian state on Palestinian territory to accommodate the far smaller number of people forced out by Israeli military action and the deliberate ethnic cleansing unleashed in the campaigns of 1948. Some 700,000 Palestinians lost their homes after the attacks on Israel following the decision of the UN to set up the Jewish state. Israel absorbed the same number of Jews driven from their ancestral land and homes by the nationalist Arab regimes that took power after 1945. That Israeli leaders used the Arab military attacks to expand Israeli land-holding at the expense of local people, and did so with brutality and cruelty, has long been exposed by Israeli historians. But why after 1948, Egypt and Jordan did not help create a Palestinian state with a capital in East Jerusalem or why the oil-rich Gulf states did not help finance a new life for the suffering Palestinians has never been explored or explained.

If there is a 'new history' in Israel on the creation of the Israeli state, is it not time we had a new history in Arab countries on their failure to support a Palestinian state in the years before the 1967 war fundamentally changed the argument? Critics of Israel have no shortage of material freely made available in Israeli archives and the open discussion of Israeli politicians, generals and state agents. This, combined with the independent historical work and political analysis of Israeli universities and policy institutes, allows the production of enormous literature critical of Israel's behaviour vis-à-vis Palestinians. Alas, there is no equivalent openness or independence in Egyptian, Jordanian, Syrian, Iranian or other relevant universities, or amongst their political leaders, generals and policy-makers. Brave individuals like the Egyptian politicial scientist Professor Saad Eddin Ibrahim have challenged the status quo thinking, but have suffered imprisonment and physical privation as a result. We are still waiting for one major Arab historian or writer who is prepared, like Benny Morris did when he demythologised the founding myths of Israel, to say that from Nasser to Arafat, from the dictator of a Syrian republic to the monarchs of

Jordan and Saudi Arabia, the Arab position on Israel has been a self-defeating disaster.

Until recently, world leaders also took little interest in the need to create a Palestinian state. In his memoirs, former French president Valéry Giscard d'Estaing recalls that in 1980 France insisted there should be no reference to a 'Palestinian state' in a European Community declaration. We can expect little better from the Gaullist traditions of Middle East politics, but the arrival in 2007 of Nicolas Sarkozy as France's president and Bernard Kouchner as France's foreign minister opens tantalising possibilities. Opportunities are there for a French Middle East policy that can lead Europe out of its impasse of paying for Palestinian development projects while having no influence over Palestinian politics, and having the worst of all worlds with Israel – namely, failure by the EU to rebuke or criticise Israel when both are justified and necessary; and silence or mealy-mouthed responses when Israel is threatened by bombs and missiles paid for by foreign powers. Today, seventy years after the first explicit call for a Palestinian state, the Palestinians are still waiting. Both Israeli Jews and Palestinian Arabs are seized by Sir Walter Scott's lament.

> Breathes there the man with soul so dead
> Who never to himself hath said,
> This is my own, my native land.
> Whose heart hath ne'er within him burn'd
> As home his footsteps he hath turn'd
> From wandering on a foreign strand?

It is antisemitism itself in its many different forms that prevents the creation of the two sovereign states for Jews and Arabs that Bill Deedes hailed in the 1930s. Israel never can feel secure as long as antisemitism in its different manifestations, expressed by Islamists in the East and intellectuals in the West – the antisemitism of the suicide bomber as well as the *salonnier* and seminar participant – remains an organising force. Equally, Palestinians will not secure justice and the right to a stable state until they reject the ideology of antisemitism. An end to antisemitism may seem an impossible demand, an unrealisable dream, but until progressive and democratic politics everywhere say a clear 'No' to antisemitism, in all its variations, there is little hope of justice for the Palestinians and peace on the eastern shores of the Mediterranean.

Britain shut its doors to Jewish immigration at the beginning of the twentieth century. The Polish government in the 1920s nationalised industries in which many Jews made a living and forced the replacement of Jewish Polish workers by Catholic Poles. This policy of Polish jobs for Polish (Catholic) workers created a new push for Jewish emigration in response to the antisemitism of the Polish state. The United States initiated a two-decade-long policy of refusing to take Jewish immigrants in 1924. This forced Jews emigrating from poverty, pogroms and antisemitic politics in old Europe to look not to the new world but to Palestine. The antisemitism behind banning Jewish immigration into the US and west Europe was thus the main driving force behind the arrival of European Jews in Palestine. After 1945, the antisemitic ethnic-cleansing politics of the rulers of countries like Egypt and Iraq, which had long been home to major Jewish populations, led to further waves of Jewish emigration to Israel. The Iraqi Jew Naim Kattan, in his memoir *Farewell Babylon*, describes the rise of antisemitism in Iraq in the 1940s. 'Every year our chances dwindled and the screws were put on our prospects for the future. My uncle was enraged when he was refused admission to the Faculty of Medicine . . . We had pitched our tents on this land from time immemorial', but for the Iraqi government, Jews were not wanted and hundreds of thousands left for Israel or where they might be safe. They have no right of return to their homes in Iraq in which they lived for centuries.

Today's Polish government recognises no right of return for Germans driven off their ancestral land in Silesia or East Prussia after 1945. The Czech government makes no apology for the Benes decrees, which treated Sudeten Germans far worse than the Palestinians expelled in the fighting that took place when Arab states ill-advisedly sought to snuff out the Israeli state after its existence was declared by the United Nations. If there is a right of return for every displaced Palestinian, why not for the much more numerous displaced Germans? Do Jews have a right of return to Alexandria, Cairo, Tunis or Baghdad?

A century ago, the Jewish or Zionist desire for a nation and a state they controlled was like the Irish desire to be masters of their destiny. Herzl and Weizmann have much in common with de Valera. They were stubborn visionaries who refused the compromises that denied them their nation and their state. Israel is one of the expressions of the 'spring-time of nations' − begun in the middle of the nineteenth century and still not ended. The British may have produced the Balfour Declaration, but of equal historic weight was the similar declaration by France's foreign minister, Jules Cambon, which was published several months before the Balfour statement. France solemnly offered 'recognition to the Jewish nationality on the land from which the people of Israel were driven centuries ago'. It was not the Balfour Declaration that encouraged Jews to settle in Palestine, however, but the Aliens Act of the early twentieth century, which shut England's door to Jews fleeing violence further east in Europe.

Churchill warned Lloyd George against putting Jews in his Cabinet. Two decades later he warned the House of Commons in 1946 against 'a vast dumping of the Jews of Europe into Palestine'. British officials ignored the wishes of Palestinian Arabs in the 1920s and imposed a virulent Jew-hater and Nazi sympathiser as Grand Mufti of Jerusalem, even if that city had always enjoyed a majority of Jewish inhabitants under the Ottoman empire.

Papers like the *Daily Express* and *Daily Mail* campaigned in the 1930s to prevent Jews fleeing Nazism from coming to England. The *Daily Mail*'s proprietor, Lord Rothermere, was an early proponent of one of the enduring expressions of antisemitism – the belief that a Jewish lobby controls a nation's policy. He congratulated Hitler on 'freeing the country from the Israelites of international attachment who had insinuated themselves into key positions in the German administrative machine'. In August 1938, the *Daily Mail* whipped up British antisemitism with editorials that declared: 'The way stateless Jews from Germany are pouring into every port of this country is becoming an outrage.' As with today's hate and intolerance against immigrants, refugees from political violence and Europeans from the poor countries of the EU, the popular press in Britain fomented antisemitism in the first half of the last century. America was little better. Henry Ford, the creator of mass-consumption capitalism, was a roaring Jew-hater in the immediate aftermath of the First World War. He published a series of articles, later collected as a book, *The International Jew: The World's Foremost Problem*. Ford also widely distributed the antisemitic tract *The Protocols of the Elders of Zion*. It is too often forgotten that American antisemitism was as virulent as its European forebear. Franklin Delano Roosevelt was often called 'Jewsvelt' by his conservative opponents. Of course, America did not expel Jews, but the US authorities were keen to deport back to European countries left-wing Jewish activists in the first of the anti-left witch-hunts of the early 1920s. And the decision to ban Jewish immigration into America in 1924 was as antisemitic an act as any to be found in the European democracies.

Britain's post-war foreign secretary Ernest Bevin was hostile to the creation of a Jewish state. To its shame, Britain abstained at the United Nations when the existence of Israel as a member state of the United Nations was agreed. Bevin told the Labour Party conference in 1946 that American support for allowing Holocaust survivors to enter Palestine 'was proposed from the purest of motives. They did not want too many Jews in New York.' The Foreign Office sustained its antisemitism by placing articles in the Arab press. These were ostensibly written by Arab journalists, though, in fact, prepared in London. British propagandists wove together two favourite themes – the Jews and the Communists. Foreign Office officials wrote articles for the Arab press arguing that the creation of Israel was a Soviet 'plot' to dominate the region, much as today antisemites argue that Israel is an American-financed incubus in the Middle East. One Foreign Office article argued:

> It can safely be assumed that no pathetic refugee 'hungering for Zion' who sails with Russian permission and connivance from a Russian-controlled port or filters mysteriously though the Russian zone in Europe on his way to Palestine, departs without Russian approval as a reliable exponent of the Soviet ideology which Russia intends to impose on this Arab world.

British officials tried to stop the grandfather of the present foreign secretary, David Miliband, from re-entering Britain as a Jewish asylum seeker after the Second World War.

So for antisemites the establishment of a Jewish home, then state, on the shores of the Mediterranean moves from being a British imperial conspiracy to a Soviet plot and today is ascribed to a powerful Jewish lobby in the United States. Geneva-based Islamist Said Ramadan, father of the contemporary Islamist Tariq Ramadan, wrote in 1964 of a

> Jewish plot . . . It is no accident that the state of Israel was created. We are convinced that in reality it is the incarnation of a hellish thinking, a mixture born of the meeting between greedy Zionism . . . such as took form in *The Protocols of the Elders of Zion* and the spirit of the Crusades, inspired by jealousy of and hate against Islam.

The simple notion that Jews might themselves, by themselves, of and for themselves want a state they could call their own seems too difficult a concept to understand.

As we have seen in the previous chapter it is easier to blame cabals wielding occult influence over world affairs. The French historian and philosopher Pierre-André Taguieff has written a short book, *L'imaginaire du Complot Mondial*, which examines modernity's need to believe in secret conspiracies and plots that explain what is really happening in the world. At a banal level, expression of this belief in secret forces dictating world history can be found in Dan Brown's novels or TV series like *The X-Files*. But for many, the belief in the occult powers and influence of secretive Jewish networks remains central. An academic from the University of East Anglia, Dr Lee Marsden, wrote to *The Guardian* in September 2007 about 'the Israel lobby'. As with Mearsheimer and Walt in America (discussed in chapter 8) it is taken as a given in many left-liberal circles that an all-encompassing Jewish lobby is plotting around the clock in

Britain to stifle any discussion of the Middle East other than along lines pleasing to the Israeli government. Mubarak Chameki, vice president of the Libyan People's Assembly, told a meeting in April 2006: 'The real terrorism is part of a plot aimed at Islam. This plot has different faces and the defamation of the Prophet by cartoonists is one aspect of it.' At the same conference in Iran, Bahreini politician Fakhra Diara explained that 'the Zionist International' lay behind the problems Palestinians face. The same need to conjure up secret lobbies, internationals and conspiracies and plots to explain the Middle East imbroglio lies behind the claims that no Jews were killed when the World Trade Center towers were destroyed or that Mossad or the CIA had secretly organised the attack to discredit Muslims. At a meeting with Muslim leaders in Yorkshire in my constituency of Rotherham in October 2001, I heard senior representatives of the Muslim community, amongst them doctors, accountants and businessmen, announce that no Jew reported for work on the morning of the 9/11 attack and that in reality the attack had been secretly planned by Jews to discredit Islam. I looked at faces hoping to find someone ready to laugh away such nonsense. But heads nodded in agreement around the room. When belief in plots and secret influence takes over, it is hard to reinstate rationality.

The defeat of Nazism did not eradicate antisemitism from Europe. In December 1946, George Orwell wrote a short essay on the best-selling novel *Trilby*, by George du Maurier. It was published in 1894 and introduced the character Svengali to English readers. Orwell notes,

the most interesting thing about [the novel] is the different impressions one derives from reading it first before and then after the career of Hitler . . . There is no question that the book is antisemitic. Apart from the fact that Svengali's vanity, treachery, selfishness, personal uncleanliness and so forth are constantly connected with the fact that he is a Jew, there are the illustrations [these were also done by du Maurier, who drew for *Punch*]. [H]e made Svengali into a sinister caricature of the traditional type.

Orwell argues that while the book is antisemitic, du Maurier presents Svengali as cleverer than the Englishmen he shares the novel with.

It is the attitude of the rugger-playing prefect towards the spectacled 'swot', and it was probably the normal attitude towards Jews at that time. They were natural inferiors, but of course they were cleverer, more sensitive and more artistic than ourselves, because such qualities are of secondary importance. Nowadays the English are less sure of themselves, less confident that stupidity always wins in the end, and the prevailing form of antisemitism has changed, not altogether for the better.

A month later, Orwell noted that antisemitism had become 'discreditable, and so the scapegoat is sought elsewhere'. For Orwell, the Poles, who had arrived en masse in Britain after 1940 and could not return to their Communist-run country, were now the object of 'race hatred'. Dislike of Poles, he wrote, 'is the contemporary equivalent of antisemitism'. It is a commonplace to note that antisemitism is an expression of racism. When it is no longer permitted to attack Jews, then other immigrants will do. But while antisemitism is indeed racist, it is more serious and worse in its implications. Racism can be countered. Discrimination against black or Asian Britons can be made illegal. Help can be given to promote people from ethnic minorities. Economic development and access to education can be targeted to overcome or lessen racism. But Jew-hatred easily segues into Israel-hatred. The kind of collective guilt imposed on Jews by earlier anti-semites is now imposed on all Jews in Israel and family and friends living in Europe or America irrespective of whether they approve of the actions of the democratically elected government of Israel or not.

Immediately after 1945, however, antisemitism had indeed become in Orwell's phrase 'discreditable' and it remained discreditable for some time to come. The antisemitism of nineteenth-century Europe, and the antisemitic refusal of the United States in the 1920s and 1930s to allow Jewish immigration, as well as the appeasement and refusal to take steps to confront fascism in Spain, Italy or Germany on the part of the Euro-Atlantic democracies gave rise to the determination of Jews to have their own state and defend it and its citizens from attacks by Arab armies in 1948 through to bombs and missile attacks in this century. Had Europe been able to confront its antisemitism and deny it political oxygen, then Israel would not have come into existence as it did in 1948.

Today, all the arguments of European antisemitism have been taken over as a job lot by Islamist and Arab anti-semitism. From dissemination of *The Protocols of the Elders of Zion* to the repetition of the European belief in Jewish lobbies dictating policy or controlling the professions, media and financial networks there is very little new in contemporary Islamist or Arab antisemitism. A study by Professor Denis MacEoin of Newcastle University, published in 2007, into the material available at mosque bookshops and Muslim schools in Britain found this document made available to students:

Some Examples of the Methods Employed by Zionism to Accomplish its Goals

1. Instigating confusion, schemes and conspiracies throughout history . . . You will not find any confusion in which the Jews did not play a role.
2. Their attempt at trying to immerse nations in vice and the spread of fornication. The Jews controlled this kind of trade and promoted it. They manage the bars in Europe and the United States and in Israel itself.
3. Controlling literature and art by spreading immoral pornographic literature.
4. Controlling the movie industry and art in the Western world and elsewhere.
5. Cheating, bribing, stealing and conning.

The Jews are a people who were moulded with treachery and backstabbing throughout the centuries and they will not keep their word nor honour their promise.

Colin Cook, a Muslim convert, who taught for eighteen years at the King Fahd academy in London, has revealed that pupils at the school, which is funded and controlled by the Saudi Arabian government, were taught from Arabic books that likened Jews to 'monkeys' and 'pigs'.

How young British Muslims are expected to move towards a politics of supporting Israel's right to exist and of peace between Jews and Muslims in the Middle East while they are exposed to this hate literature is hard to see. When MacEoin's scrupulous, rigorously sourced report was published, the Muslim Council of Britain (MCB) did not move swiftly to rid British mosque bookshops of this poisonous material. (In addition to Jew-hating antisemitic texts there are masses of material on offer to young British Muslims inveighing against women's rights or gays as well as inviting them to jihad and martyrdom.) On the contrary, the MCB attacked both the message and the messenger and dismissed the MacEoin report. The MCB is still seeking to return as a privileged partner of the British government on Muslim issues, which the organisation once had in the first period of the Labour government. As long as the MCB turns a blind eye to anti-semitic, misogynist and homophobe material, and sees no problem in the presence of this literature in the bookshops and schools of Britain's Muslim community then its status has to be questioned, not endorsed. To its shame, the BBC *Newsnight* programme sought to discredit and defame the research carried out, instead of exposing the anti-Jewish and other hate literature made available by Islamists within Britain.

If the argument can be made that without antisemitism Israel would not have come into existence, there is now no chance of achieving the proclaimed dream of many Islamists for the eradication of the state of Israel. But the rights of the Palestinians to live in peace on their own land are severely threatened by post-1945 antisemitism as it has arisen as a guiding ideology for many. The more antisemitism resurfaces, the more Israel and Jews will become stubborn and unable to contemplate compromises with forces judged to be using the same arguments as classic antisemites. And Palestinian supporters in the Euro-Atlantic democracies do their cause no service by making the same analogies about Jewish power, lobbies, influence, wealth and reach into government as did the Jew-haters of old. It is not until the cause of Palestinian rights is divorced from antisemitism that it will fully flourish. Old antisemitism gave birth to Israel. Neo-antisemitism makes Israel more determined than ever. Until all traces of antisemitism, especially the disguised forms that infect Western political activism, are seen to be opposed then the hopes for peace in the Middle East will not be realised.

Anti-antisemitism is now a political priority. The unyielding right in Israel who believe they have their God's permission to create an ever-expanding Israel wherever they wish, their neo-conservative and fundamentalist supporters in America and the Islamophobe Israel-right-or-wrong groups in Europe all feed on antisemitism and anti-Zionism. Those who want peace based on a secure Israel and a coexisting Palestine have to start by ripping out antisemitic and anti-Zionist sentiments from their thinking. They have to make clear that the Jew-hate contained in the Hamas Charter, or in much Muslim Brotherhood thinking and writing, or given expression by the Iranian state when it sponsored the Holocaust denial conference, undermines all solidarity and support from the democratic world.

10

What Can be Done?

I love Europe's high mountains. Skiing them in the winter, climbing and walking the Alps and other mountains and hills of Europe in the summer have been the most rewarding days of my life. The last Alpine hamlet in France before one crosses into Switzerland along the road from Chamonix to Martigny is called Barberine. It is set back from the road and even today has no more than half a dozen small houses at the foot of a winding, steep, stony path that comes down from the Emosson dam looming a thousand metres higher. The track is rarely walked and no one stops as they drive across the French–Swiss frontier. In the war, Barberine was the last French village in the Alps under Nazi control, a tantalising few metres from the freedom of Switzerland. On one of the houses there is a small plaque that reads:

> *Ici de novembre 1943 à aout 1944, Pierre et Marie Devillaz ont abrité mes parents Minda-Lea et David Kipnis, juifs traqués par les Nazis. Que leur mémoire soit bénie. Leo Kipnis, 1998.* (Here between November 1943 and August 1944, Pierre and Marie Devillaz gave shelter to my parents, Minda-Lea and David Kipnis, Jews hunted by the Nazis. May their memory be blessed. Leo Kipnis, 1998.)

What Can be Done?

This French couple who, at the height of the war on the very edge of Nazi-occupied France, took two Jews into their small house in a tiny hamlet gave witness that in the darkest moment of hatred in world history, there were ordinary, poor, provincial French citizens who were ready to defy the culture of antisemitism that infected many in their country and risk the wrath of the occupier as well as the betrayal of neighbours in a part of France where the antisemitic Milice carried out cruel exactions. It is possible, therefore, to defy and to defeat antisemitism by standing up to it just as it is possible to take on the racism and xenophobia that infects such broad areas of politics and the populist media.

Antisemitism has been called a light sleeper. It is wide awake now. The antisemitism of old has morphed into something new. It is a significant component of the new ideology, one might call it the 'Endarkenment', which is seeking to de-Occidentalise the world. Many will argue that the world does not need Occidental values and that no set of values has superiority. If so, it is time to bring down the curtain on an Averroës or a Maimonides trying to explain to their respective Muslim and Jewish communities of the twelfth century that faith could walk hand in hand with reason. When Paris was liberated in 1944, General de Gaulle wrote that from 'one day to the next, one could say, read, meet as one pleased'. Those freedoms to speak, write, publish and to meet in private and public to promote competing ideas are not Occidental or Western ideas. They are universal rights of all humanity. We relativise them at our peril. How many years did I waste in left-wing meetings in which I was told that the proclaimed economic and social rights offered by communism were superior to the 'bourgeois' rights of free expression, rule of law and democratic elections? How many years have I wasted reading in Conservative newspapers that decent pay and holidays, and fair taxes to pay for health, housing and education for all were an unacceptable imposition on the rights of business and capital to do as it pleased? Rights laid down by the United Nations, or the International Labour Organisation, or in the European Charter of Fundamental Rights contained in the EU Treaty of Lisbon are for everybody – men and women, rich and poor, black and white, for all religions and colours and for me, a heterosexual, as much as my gay friends.

As I defend the right of my Muslim friends to follow their faith and support their causes how can I accept a politics that denies those to Jewish friends? Combating neo-antisemitism is not about supporting every demand made by Jews, and certainly not interpretations of Judaism that deny women or non-Jews equal rights. Still less is it an endorsement of whatever the government of Israel does or says. But to combat global antisemitism is to confront words, language and political demands that start from the premise that Israel as defined by its citizens cannot exist. In her moving book *Married to Another Man: Israel's Dilemma in Palestine*, about the plight of Palestinians expelled after 1948, the physician and writer Ghada Karmi writes of Israel 'encircling the Arab world' and declares that 'The profound damage done to the Arab world by Israel's creation is a big, untold story in the West.' Why? The Israel of today, let alone the Israel of 1948, is not responsible for what happens in Algeria or Yemen. The majority of Arab states have no common borders with Israel. In 2004, the United Nations Development Programme produced a report on 'Human Development in the Arab World'. It showed:

- Productivity in Arab countries had decreased over the past forty years; in the preceding twenty years there had been zero growth;

- 30 per cent of the Arab population live on less than two dollars a day;
- One in every two Arab women cannot read or write;
- 1 per cent of Arabs own a computer.

All this is Israel's fault? ALESCO, the Arab League Educational, Scientific and Cultural Organisation, has itself listed the barriers to cultural development in the Arab world. In addition to the fact that more books are translated into Dutch from foreign languages than are translated and published in all Arab countries, a denial of access to universal culture that ranks amongst the worst in modern times, Arabs face:

- Mass illiteracy;
- Overemphasis on patriotism;
- Administrative barriers preventing circulation of culture between countries;
- Government control over people's minds;
- Excessive use of propaganda.

Can all these be blamed on Israel? Dr Karmi does her people, her fellow Arabs and the cause of Palestine no good by seeking to make Israel the scapegoat for all the failings of every Arab government in so many spheres, over so many years. She rightly says that Israel is instrumentalised by Arab political and religious readers to cover up their own shortcomings. The answer, one might hope, would be to accept that Israel is not going to disappear and that Jews will want to live in their own state.

At some future stage, perhaps tolerance will replace hate. Coexistence under some other political dispensation may be possible. Early in 2008, I walked across the Red Sea border between the Jordanian town of Aqaba and its Israeli neighbour Eilat. The formalities were few and both Jordanian and

Israeli officials were friendly. I was partly reminded of cross-
ing into Communist east Europe from the democratic west in
the days when two ideologies glared at each other in the
middle of Europe. Yet how quickly what was taken as a
permanent state of affairs dissolved into the borderless unity
of today's European Union! Europeans who only yesterday
were at each other's throats, and demonised neighbours and
rival countries and religions, now live peacefully without
frontier controls and integrate as citizens and economic actors
under the aegis of the European Union.

It is not my purpose to paint such a rosy future for the
eastern Mediterranean region, let alone the wider Arab
world, but until some effort is made to tell the truth to
Arabs, including Palestinians, that anti-Jewish, anti-Israel
words and acts are self-defeating the hopes of a European
style of coexistence in the region will be slim. The leaders of
Jordan have shown courage in signing a peace treaty with
Israel and allowing near-normal border crossings. Yet as I set
out to stroll from Muslim Semitic Jordan into Jewish Semitic
Israel I read an article in the *Jordan Star* full of bilious hate.
The author is one John V. Whitlock, of whom I have never
heard and never want to read again. He argued that to insist
on ' "Israel's right to exist" is unreasonable, immoral and
impossible to meet'. He produced the tired argument that the
expulsion of 700,000 Palestinians between 1947 and 1949 in a
year when millions were being forcibly removed from their
ancestral homes as part of the great post-1945 settlement was
on a par with the organised, industrial, systematic, patient
murder of six million Jews using the highest technological
and logistical skills of Europe.

So while the political leaders of Jordan, including the
millions of Palestinians who live as Jordanian citizens, learn
to come to terms with Israel's existence and offer a model for

coexistence with the Jewish state, a major Jordanian paper continues to publish the hate language that poisons any hope of settlement. An end to antisemitism is the beginning of a rebirth of the Arab peoples and their nations. A defeat for Islamist jihadism and Islamist fundamentalist denial of universal rights is a necessary, if insufficient, condition for Arab democracy to come into being and replace the various forms of authoritarianism in Arab states. 'If nothing changes in their Arab homelands', writes Timothy Garton Ash, 'tens of millions of young people will want to leave the near East for the near West. If Europe does not bring more prosperity and freedom to these young Arabs, these young Arabs will come to Europe.' Garton Ash, one of the wisest of our international analysts, is right. The question is, can the prosperity and freedom for Arabs arrive without an end to the rising neo-antisemitism – even if disguised as anti-Zionism or anti-Israeli politics? If the disappearance or weakening of the tiny Jewish state is a precondition then surely the world faces a very long wait before Arabs can enjoy the prosperity or even the limited liberties of most people in Asia, without considering Europe or the Americas. Antisemitism in its varying manifestations is hate. Hope never comes into being until hate fades.

Edmund Burke noted that: 'Before men can transact any affair, they must have a common language to speak, and some common recognised principles on which they can argue; otherwise all is cross-purpose and confusion.' A consequence of neo-antisemitism and its unwitting conveyors in our politics, media and intellectual life is that it prevents the arrival of the 'common language' Burke identified as the first condition for doing positive-sum politics. I can hear and agree with my Muslim friends when they complain about Israeli brutality. But do they hear me when I say that, in exchange, they must repudiate the antisemitism of Islamist ideologues and organisations? I can agree with them that Israel must abide by UN resolutions. Will they agree with me that UN member states must allow one of their number an unconditional right to exist? If not, Burke is right. All is cross-purpose and confusion.

As the Moroccan writer Mohammed Charfi states: 'Peace and harmony will exist between individuals and between peoples once there is a clear separation between politics and religion and once we have taught our children these principles.' Across the world from those seeking to enter the White House to the caves on the Pakistan–Afghanistan border sheltering jihadi fundamentalists, Charfi's insight is repudiated as political leaders insist that religion trumps politics. The basis of old and neo-antisemitism remains the rejection of the right to be different. The right to a different religion, different culture, different ways of organising communities, different sexualities, different international solidarities, affections or affiliations. By their failure to discourage and actively oppose antisemitism within Europe's Muslim communities, the ideologues and organisers of contemporary Islamism are doing Europe's Muslims a great disservice.

In denying the right to Jewish identity, the right of Jews to live on their terms in part of the land that is as historically theirs as any Semitic race, or the right of Jews to their differences, the hardline Islamists are playing into the hands of conservative bigots and the extreme right. The latter seek popular support by playing on the fears of Islam and reject the right of European-born Muslims to be allowed to pray, eat, marry and follow customs and culture that are different. Neo-antisemitism and Islamophobia are, if not quite twin sides of the same coin, certainly produced at the same mint. In their hate language against Jews and Israelis, the ideological

Islamists and the silent number of Muslims who endorse privately their views of Jews and Israel articulate what might be called the Bonhoeffer disservice, 'When they blew up Jews in Tel Aviv, I did not protest. When they called for Rushdie's death, I did not protest. When they threatened cartoonists, I did not protest. When they came for Muslims or for Islam, there was no one left to protest.' But if you live in David Irving's and President Ahmadinejad's world of Holocaust denial, you don't know who Pastor Dietrich Bonhoeffer was.

That is why the final appeal must be to shapers of political and public opinion. Those who denounce antisemitism will not be listened to if they combine their appeals to respect Jewish identity with ranting hatred against Muslims and Islam. Somehow, somewhere, a new politics and language has to grow that replaces the mutual contradictions of today's discussion of Israel and Palestine, Jews and Muslims, by a more tolerant politics that adds value to human existence. From the point of view of a European politician like myself that cannot happen unless and until neo-antisemitism is understood, exposed and rejected by all except dyed-in-the-wool Jew-haters. There are many, like the good and noble German Social Democratic politician Gert Weisskirchen, who are beginning this fight-back in a European context. Organisations like the EU or the OSCE, which took little notice of antisemitism until recently, now recognise that neo-antisemitism is a fundamental threat to European democracy. Britain's pioneering parliamentary work against antisemitism is now being taken up by parliaments in other democratic nations. The Council of Europe remains an important part of Europe's political fight against neo-antisemitism. The work of educating young people about the Holocaust continues to grow. Gordon Brown, when

Chancellor, provided funds for thousands of young British students to visit the end stations of anti-Jewishism, anti-Zionism and antisemitism, namely the single-line rail tracks that come to an end in a far-away field in eastern Europe with just the doors of a gas chamber waiting to open. There are many inter-faith groups hard at work. Intellectuals like Saad Eddin Ibrahim in Cairo need encouragement and support at the highest international level. Britain's Christian, Muslim and Jewish leaders meet and important theological work is under way to rescue Islam from literalist interpretations, as those religious fundamentalists who deform politics whether in North America, Europe, Israel or in Muslim nations and communities are equally dangerous.

I began my political engagement more than three decades ago by wanting to combat the racism I could see in the working-class communities of the West Midlands where I moved to work as a young BBC reporter. That led me to my natural home on the democratic reformist left as, on the whole, it has been the progressive-democratic-left family in politics that has been in the forefront of combating racism. I wish I was confident that was true about combating the twenty-first-century variety of racism, neo-antisemitism. Nonetheless, I am confident that democracy and universal human values will triumph over antisemitism, misogyny, denial of free expression and homophobia. Racism has not been defeated, still less intolerance. But the fight is always worthwhile. And, in having to write this book, I have to conclude that the struggle never ends, nor does the duty, in Auden's words, to 'show an affirming flame'.

Acknowledgements

This book originates from my work chairing the All Party Parliamentary Inquiry into Antisemitism in 2005 and 2006. I am grateful to John Mann MP for inviting me to set up and chair the inquiry. The following MPs served on the Inquiry and I am grateful for their continuing support on the important task of combating antisemitism: Rt Hon Kevin Barron MP; Tim Boswell MP; Rt Hon David Curry MP; Rt Hon Iain Duncan Smith MP; Nigel Evans MP; Rt Hon Bruce George MP; Lady Sylvia Hermon MP; Chris Huhne MP; Daniel Kawczynski MP; Barbara Keeley MP; Khalid Mahmood MP; Rt Hon John Spellar MP; and Theresa Villiers MP. Different people in different ways have helped with writing this book including Elliot Conway, Maurice Jones, Collin Gonze, Amy Philip, Sadie Smith, Jardena Lande, Richard Angell, Clarissa Hyman, Lord Greville Janner, Axelle Lemaire, the Rt Hon Sir Gerald Kaufman MP, Joan Smith, Sir Michael Pakenham and Vernon Bogdanor. I am grateful to the House of Commons Library for their help with documentation and books, and to colleagues on the Council of Europe's Parliamentary Assembly. Bea Hemming and Alan Samson have been terrific editors. George Weidenfeld encouraged me as he has done so many over decades of service to the cause of freedom and democracy. Britain owes a massive debt to Lord Weidenfeld, *un éditeur et un Européen sans peur et sans reproche.* I would like to dedicate this book to the memory of Herman Rebhan, a socialist Jew from Cologne who came to America in 1938 to serve in the United Autoworkers Union and then as an international trade union leader in the 1980s when apartheid, communism and military rule in Latin America and in Asia were all defeated thanks to the work of democratic trade unions which Herman Rebhan supported as a social democrat and in the best traditions of Jewish humanism. I had the privilege of working with him. He was a European Jew driven into exile by antisemitism as millions of his fellow Jews perished. *Nie wieder,* say today's Germans – Never again – and the battle against twenty-first-century anti-semitism is as important as the battle against its twentieth-century version.

Notes and References

vii *'antisemitism cannot be banned'*: Raphael, p. 6.

viii *'nosological approach'*: Steven Beller, *Antisemitism. A Very Short Introduction*, Oxford, OUP, 2007, pp. 4–5.

viii *'the answer to antisemitism'*: ibid., p. 119.

viii *summer of 2005*: Report of the All-Party Parliamentary Inquiry into Antisemitism.

ix *'Islam will not arrive'*: Meddeb, p. 27.

xi *'sickness of Islam'*: ibid., p. 82.

xi *wartime Tunisia*: ibid., p. 212. xi *'modern Islamic* militancy': Burke.

xi *'confusion'*: Parliamentary Assembly of the Council of Europe Resolution 1605, 2008

xi *'Central to leading'*: Sen, p. xiii.

1 *Jews need 'to be perfected'*: Newsweek, 18 February 2008.

4 *'origins of the French president'*: Libération, 29 November 2007.

7 *'armed resistance'*: London Review of Books, 20 September 2007.

7 *'cast doubts'*: The Times, 3 October 2007.

9 *antisemitic incidents*: Community Security Trust Report, 31 July 2008.

13 *'military gains*: Shlomo Ben-Ami, *Scars of War, Wounds of Peace: The Israel-Arab Tragedy*, London, Weidenfeld & Nicolson, 2006, p. 36.

14 *engage with Hamas*: Halevy, p. 277.

15 *'killing millions of people'*: International Herald Tribune, 29 September 2007.

16 *'Hannah Arendt'*: Hitchens, p. 251.

19 *'offensive question about Jews'*: Alan Clark, *Diaries: Into Politics*, Phoenix, 2001, p. 309.

20 *Hugh Dalton*: Beckett, p. 145.

21 *'John Beckett'*: ibid., p. 54.

21 *'Mond was corrupt'*: ibid.

21 *Conservative Home Secretary*: Lebzelter, p.167.

21 *first-ever Jewish Conservative MP*: Harry Defries, *Conservative Party Attitudes to Jews 1900–1950*, Frank Cass, 2001, pp. 208–9.

21 *'Your ambassador'*: Greville Janner, *To Life! The Memoirs of Greville Janner*, Sutton Publishing, 2006, p. 193.

21 *1970 election*: Stephen Brook. *The Club: The Jews of Modern Britain*, Constable, 1996, p. 395.

22 *'anti-Jewish insinuation'*: personal conversation with author.

22 *Gerry Healey 'blatant anti-Semite'*: Andrew Hosken, *Ken*, Arcadia, 2008, p. 127.

22 *Reg Freeson: Sunday Telegraph*, 12 March 2000.23 *'Jewish bitch'*: King, pp. 261–2.

23 *'antisemitism was another factor'*: evidence to All-Party Parliamentary Inquiry into Antisemitism, op. cit.

25 *'dangerous game'*: *Evening Standard*, 2 March 2006.

26 *'Conservative Party was antisemitic'*: Hosken, pp. 386–99.

27 *secret power of the Jews*: John Tyndall, *The Eleventh Hour*, 1988, quoted in John Tyndall, *Do We Need Jewish Candidates?*, 2004.

27 *'organised Jewry'*: ibid.

28 *Griffin pamphlet*: Nick Griffin, *Who Are the Mindbenders?*, British National Party publication, 1997.

31 *Stoyanov*: *Daily Telegraph* interview with Stoyanov quoted in *Searchlight*, 380, February 2007.

32 *Radio Maryja*: 'Poland: Democracy and the Challenge of Extremism', Anti-Defamation League, New York, 2006.

34 *'Germans did not invent antisemitism'*: a good summary of recent books, research projects and opinion polls on German antisemitism can be found in the collection of papers in *Antisemitismus* edited by Sabine Klingelhöfer, in *Aus Politik und Zeitgeschichte*, Berlin, July 2007, on which some of this chapter is based.

34 *'Antisemitism? Antizionism? Criticism of Israel?'*: Press Notice of German Foreign Ministry (Auswärtiges Amt), Berlin, August 2007.

38 *a fifth of all German students*: A. Zick and B. Küpper *Antisemitismus in Deutschland und Europa*, in Klingelhöfer, op. cit., p. 12.

39 *six forms of anti-Semitism*: ibid.

40 *Horst Mahler*: Rainer Erb, *Organisierte Antisemiten*, in ibid., p. 21.

42 *Antizionism must not be confused with anti-Semitism*: Winock, p. 352.

42 *'punishment of Zionist criminals'*: ibid., p. 175.

Notes and References

42 *'conquering Israeli'*: ibid., p. 177.

43 *Darquier de Pellepoix*: Wieviorka, p. 39.

43 *'invented massacre of Jews'*: ibid.

45 *Garaudy to Cairo*: Le Point, 22 March 2007.

45 *Sheik Tantawi has*: BBC News, 11 July 2003.

45 *Pascal Boniface*: Wieviorka, p. 54.

46 *Stéphane Zagdanski and Theo Klein*: Nouvel Observateur, 23 May 2006.

47 *L'Oréal*: see Waitzfelder, 2008.

48 *'He is the real right'*: Le Monde, 27 April 2006.

48 *'funny'*: Libération, 22 December 2006.

50 *Argentina*: Martina Libertad Weisz, 'Continuity and Change in Argentinian Antisemitism', in *Antisemitism International*, No. 3–4, 2006, Hebrew University, Jerusalem.

54 *'They're not burning synagogues'*: Miami Herald, 19 May 2007.

56 *Jewish 'shadow world government'*: David Goodman, 'The Protocols of the Elders of Zion, Aum and antisemitism in Japan', in *Antisemitism International*, op. cit.

59 *'Islamist control'*: Husain, pp. 145–6.

59 *'Islam: The Final Solution'*: ibid., p. 54–5.

60 *Scottish Universities*: Herald, 20 July 2005.

61 *'NUS ban'*: ibid.

62 *DeLong-Bas, Massad, Bazian*: www.campus-watch.org

63 *'worldwide Jewish supremacism'*: Chesler, p. 144.

63 *Jews=Nazis*: ibid.

63 *sacralised misogyny*: ibid., p. 163.

63 *'Israel Arabs'*: ibid.

64 *'Promoting Good Campus Relations'*: All-Party Inquiry into Antisemitism: Government Responses, One Year On Progress Report, UK Government Command Paper 738, The Stationery Office, London, May 2008.

69 *'Stalin was an anti-semite'*: Tony Judt, *Postwar: A History of Europe*, London, Heinemann, 2005, p. 1.

70 *'Anti-Jewish feelings'*: ibid., p. 775.

81 *'If you were to ask me'*: Report of the All-Party Parliamentary Inquiry into Antisemitism, henceforth *APPIIAS*, p. 1.

81 *Henry Grunwald*: ibid., p. 2.

81 *'grinding low level of antisemitism'*: ibid.

83 *Zionism as a political movement*: see Wheatcroft, 1996, for a very thoughtful and thorough account of Zionism.

84 *sought to chide Paulin*: Jonathan Freedland, 'Is Anti-Zionism antisemitism?', in Paul Iganski and Barry Kosman, eds, *A New*

Antisemitism? Debating Judeophobia in 21st-Century Britain', London, Profile Books, pp. 113–29.

85 *Kosher Conspiracy: New Statesman*, 14 January 2002.

87 *Guardian published an image: Guardian*, 19 July 2006.

87 *Guardian apologised: Guardian*, 22 July 2006.

78 *Mikhal Nazarov:* www.soldat.ru, 1 August 2006.

91 *text from Dante:* Ruthven, pp. 2–3.

91 *'Islamic fundamentalism':* ibid., p. 99.

92 *'Embedded in the anti-Western thrust':* ibid., p. 101.

93 *Souri:* see Kepel, 2008.

94 *'The Muslim Community':* Hasan al-Banna, *Tractates*, quoted in Ronald Nettler, *Past Trials and Present Tribulations. A Muslim Fundamentalist's View of the Jews*, Oxford, Pergamon Press, 1987, p. 18.

95 *stoning women to death: Daily Telegraph*, 10 November 2007. 95 *'a woman was stoned to death':* Royal Society of Arts debate, 13 November 2007.

95 *Professor Küng asks: Islam: Past, Present and Future*, One World, Oxford, 2007.

95 *'Renewal always takes place':* ibid., p. 542.

96 *'reject . . . reason, rationality':* ibid., p. 541.

96 *'The American girl':* Sayyid Qutb, 'America I Saw', quoted in Gove, p. 20.

97 *'Jazz':* ibid.

98 *'The Jews feel':* Nettler, op. cit., p. 59.

99 *'The enmity of the Jews':* ibid., p. 59.

99 *'The Muslims expelled them':* ibid., p. 66.

99 *'This Jewish consensus':* ibid., p. 78.

99 *'This is a war':* ibid, p. 82.

100 *'Today the struggle':* ibid., p. 85.

100–1 *'The Jews have instilled':* Sayyid Qutb, 'In the Shadow of the Koran', in Olivier Carré, *Mystique et politique: Lecture révolutionnaire du Coran par Sayid Qutb, Frère musulman radical*, Paris, Éditions du Cerf et Presses de la Fondation nationale des sciences politiques, 1984, pp. 118–19, quoted in Taguieff, pp. 146–7.

102 *Abu Luqman:* Husain, p. 171.

102 *'I should have known better':* ibid.

103 *Wahhabi Jew-hatred:* ibid., p. 249.

103 *'Islamist apologists':* ibid., p. 251.

104 *'What happened to the Muslims?':* ibid., p. 252.

104 *'No, no':* ibid, p. 257.

109 *Matzo of Zion:* Mustafa Tlass, Damascus, 1983 (reprinted many times since).

Notes and References

111 *'Young Muslim women'*: Hamel, p. 22.

111 *Banna insisted*: Fourest, p. 38.

111–12 *If the German Reich'*: ibid.

112 *'is the armed struggle'*: O. Carré and M. Seurat, *Les Frères musulmans*, Paris, Gallimard, 1988, p. 45, quoted in Fourest, p. 49.

113 *'a faith-promoting narrative'*: Malise Ruthven, *New York Review of Books*, 16 August 2007.

113 *'Mohammed's leadership*: ibid.

113 *University of Geneva*: see Hamel, pp. 216–19, for a detailed study of the history of Ramadan's doctoral thesis, which saw some of the most eminent Francophone scholars of Arab and Muslim history resign from the jury rather than award a doctorate. It is hard to imagine any British or American university proceeding along the lines of Geneva University, where political influence appears to have been decisive in accepting work presented for a doctoral thesis.

114 *'not a professor'*: Hamel, p. 220.

114 *'I accept laws'*: Fourest, p. 224.

114 *'No declaration'*: ibid., p. 225.

114 *Ramadan again refuses*: NYRB, op. cit.

115 *Ramadan listed*: see Kepel, *Fitna*, pp. 376–86, for a good discussion of the controversy in the French left after Ramadan identified as Jews socialists who did not share his views.

116 *After 9/11*: Le Monde, 3 October 2001.

116 *Muslims in Lyon*: Lyon Mag October 2001, quoted in Fourest, p. 294.

116 *Panorama*: Fourest, p. 294.

116 *Oxford University*: 30 October 2007, European Studies Centre, St Antony's College, Oxford.

118 *'You are a fascist'*: Fourest, p. 340.

119 *'Homosexuality is not permitted'*: Fourest, p. 208.

120 *'The peril of Islamism'*: 'Y a-t-il un péril islamiste', conference organised by Tariq Ramadan and Alain Gresh, quoted in Fourest, p. 330.

122 *liberal rabbi*: Hamel, pp. 266–7.

126 *'The Jews are responsible*: Mel Gibson's remarks made 7 August 2006 were widely reported.

126 *Billy Graham*: Nixon Tapes quoted in *New York Times*, 1 March 2002.

128 *'eighty-five per cent'*: Mearsheimer and Walt, p. 188.

128 *'Sayyid Qutb'*: ibid., p. 65.

129 *For Hamas*: Hamas Charter from www.palestinecenter.org. There

is also a good French translation of the Hamas Charter, but the broad lines of its Jew-hating politics are the same in all languages.

129 *'there is no solution'*: Hamas Charter, Article 13.

130 *'The Nazism of the Jews'*: Hamas Charter, Article 20.

132 *Hezbollah's project*: quoted in Saad-Ghorayeb, p. 150.

132 *Jews connived with the Nazis*: ibid., p. 182.

132 *Naim Qasim*: ibid., p. 174.

133 *'the party insists'*: ibid.

134 *'tactical measures'*: Mearsheimer and Walt, p. 283.

135 *nuclear arms race*: see Francois Heisbourg, *Iran, le choix des armes?*, Paris, Stock, 2007, p. 171.

135 *knowledge of Israel*: The Nation, 15 May 2006.

136 *Arab Department*: quoted in S. Ben-Ami, op. cit., p. 43.

138 *powerful book*: Gove, p. 123.

140 *Disraeli*: Encyclopaedia Britannica, 10th edition, 1902, London, p. 481.

141 *'The Jews, however'*: ibid., p. 471.

141 *'So far from injuring the Jews'*: ibid., p. 482.

143 *Peel Commission*: W.F. Deedes, *Selected Journalism 1931–2006*, Macmillan, 2006, p. 280.

144 *'The EU showed'*: London Review of Books, 20 December 2007.

146 *'a Palestinian state'*: V. Giscard d'Estaing, *Le Pouvoir et la vie*. Vol. 3: *Choisir*, Compagnie 12, Paris, 2006, p. 344.

147 *Iraqi Jew*: N. Kattan, *Farewell Babylon*, London, Souvenir Press, 2007, p. 59.

148 *Jules Cambon*: Cambon declaration, 4 June 1917 in Y. Manor, *Naissance du sionisme politique*, Paris, Gallimard, 1981, p. 353.

149 *'a vast dumping'*: House of Commons, 1 August 1946.

149 *British antisemitism*: Daily Mail, 20 August 1938.

150 *'purest of motives'*: Alan Bullock, *Ernest Bevin: Foreign Secretary*, Heinemann, 1983, p. 277.

   two favourite themes: quoted in Peter Weiler, *British Labour and the Cold War*, Stanford University Press, Stanford, 1988, p. 208.

151 *'Jewish plot'*: quoted in Taguieff, p. 156.

152 *'the Zionist International'*: ibid., p. 177.

   Svengali: George Orwell, *Collected Essays, Letters and Journalism, 1945–1950*, Penguin, London, 1968, p. 292.

153 *Dislike of Poles*: ibid., p. 316.

154 *Newcastle University*: D. MacEoin, *The Hijacking of British Islam*, London, Policy Exchange, 2007.

155 *Colin Cook*: The Times, 15 April 2008.

158 *Barbarine*: Gabriel Grandjacques, *La Montagne-Refuge: Les Juifs au Pays du Mont-Blanc*, Montemlian, La Fontaine de Siloè, 2007.

Notes and References

160 *Plight of Palestinians*: Ghada Karmi, *Married to Another Man: Israel's Dilemma in Palestine*, London, Pluto Press, 2007, p. 35.

162 *John V. Whitlock*: *Jordan Star*, 27 December 2007.

163 *'If nothing changes'*: Garton Ash, p. 153.

164 *Moroccan writer*: Charfi, p. 250.

Select Bibliography

Education on the Holocaust and on Anti-semitism, an Overview and Analysis of Educational Approaches, Published by the OSCE Office for Democratic Institutions and Human Rights (ODIHR), 2006.

Hate Crime, 2007 Survey, Published by Human Rights First, New York, 2007.

Report of the All-Party Parliamentary Inquiry Into Antisemitism, All-Party Group Against Antisemitism, London: The Stationery Office Limited, September 2006.

Abitbol, Michel, *Juifs et Arabes au XX siècle*, Paris: Perrin, 2006.

Badinter, Robert, *Un antisémitisme ordinaire, Vichy et les avocats juifs (1940-1944)*, France: Fayard, 1997.

Beckett, Francis, *The Rebel Who Lost His Cause, The Tragedy of John Beckett MP*, London: London House, 1999.

Beinin, Joel, *The Dispersion of Egyptian Jewry*, Cairo, New York: The American University in Cairo Press, 2005.

Blanrue, Paul-Éric, *Le Monde Contre Soi*, Paris: Éditions Blanche, 2007.

Brauman, Rony and Finkielkraut, Alain, *La Discorde: Israël-Palestine, les Juifs, la France*, France: Mille et Une Nuits, 2006.

Brook, Stephen, *The Club - The Jews of Modern Britain*, London: Constable, 1989.

Burke, Jason, *Al Qaeda: The True Story of Radical Islam*, London: Penguin Books, 2004.

Burke, Jason, *On the Road To Kandahar: Travels through Conflict in the Islamic World*, London: Penguin Books, 2006.

Byrnes, Robert F, *Anti-Semitism in Modern France*, Vol. 1: *The Prologue to the Dreyfus Affair*, New Brunswick, New Jersey: Rutgers University Press, 1950.

Cesarani, David, ed., *The Making of Modern Anglo-Jewry*, Oxford: Basil Blackwell Ltd, 1990.

Charfi Mohammed, *Islam et liberté. Le malentendu historique*, Paris: Albin Michel, 2006.

Chesler, Phyllis, *The New Anti-Semitism*, San Francisco: Jossey-Bass, 2003.

Cohen, Nick, *What's Left? How Liberals Lost Their Way*, London: Fourth Estate, 2007.

Cohen, Stuart A., *English Zionists and British Jews, The Communal Politics of Anglo-Jewry 1855-1920*, Princeton, New Jersey: Princeton University Press, 1982.

Cohn-Sherbok, Dan, *The Paradox of Anti-Semitism*, London: Continuum, 2006.

Collette, Christine, and Bird, Stephen, *Jews, Labour and the Left, 1918-48*, England: Ashgate, 2000.

Davies, Norman, *God's Playground, A History of Poland*, Oxford: Clarendon Press, 1981.

Dawkins, Richard, *The God Delusion*, London: Bantam Press, 2006.

Debray, Régis, *Supplique aux nouveaux progressistes du XXI siècle*, Paris: Gallimard, 2006.

Edelman, Todd M., *The Jews of Britain 1656-2000*, Berkeley: University of California Press, 2002.

Feldman, David, *Englishmen and Jews, Social Relations and Political Culture 1840-1914*, New Haven and London: Yale University Press, 1994.

Ferguson, Niall, *The War of the World*, London: Allen Lane, Penguin Books, 2006.

Fineberg, Simon, Samuels, Shimon, and Weitzman, Mark, eds., *Antisemitism, The Generic Hatred: Essays in Memory of Simon Wiesenthal*, London: Vallentine Mitchell, 2007

Fourest, Caroline, *Frère Tariq*, Paris: Bernard Grasset, 2004.

Garton Ash, Timothy, *Free World: Why a Crisis of the West Reveals the Opportunity of Our Time*, London: Allen Lane, Penguin Books, 2004.

Gilbert, Martin, *Churchill and the Jews*, London: Simon & Schuster UK Ltd, 2007.

Glucksmann, André, Le discours de la haine, Paris: Plon, 2004.

Gojman de Backal, Alicia, *Camisas, escudos y desfiles militares*, Mexico: Fondo de Cultura Económica, 2000.

Gove, Michael, *Celsius 7/7*, London: Weidenfeld & Nicolson, 2006.

Halevy, Efraim, *Man in the Shadows*, London: Weidenfeld & Nicolson, 2006.

Hamel, Ian, *La vérité sur Tariq Ramadan*, Lausanne: Favre, 2007.

Harris, Geoffrey, *The Dark Side of Europe, the Extreme Right Today*, Edinburgh: Edinburgh University Press, 1990.

Harrison, Bernard, *The Resurgence of Anti-Semitism*, Plymouth, England: Rowman & Littlefield Publishers, Inc., 2006.

Herf, Jeffrey, *The Jewish Enemy*, Cambridge, Mass., and London, England: The Belknap Press of Harvard University Press, 2006.

Select Bibliography

Hitchens, Christopher, *God Is Not Great: The Case Against Religion*, London: Atlantic Books, 2007.

Husain, Ed, *The Islamist*, London: Penguin, 2007.

Judt, Tony, *Postwar: A History of Europe*, London: Heinemann, 2005.

Keith, Graham, *Hatred Without a Cause? A Survey of Anti-Semitism*, Carlisle, Cumbria: Paternoster Press, 1997.

Kepel, Gilles, *The Roots of Radical Islam*, Paris: Éditions La Découverte, 1984.

Kepel, Gilles, *Fitna*, Paris: Gallimard, 2004.

Kepel, Gilles, *Terreur et Martyre*, Paris: Flammarion, 2008.

Kepel, Gilles, and Milelli, Jean-Pierre, *Al Qaeda in Its Own Words*, Cambridge, Mass.: Harvard University Press, 2008.

Khadra, Yasmina, *The Sirens of Baghdad*, London: William Heinemann, 2007.

King, Oona, *House Music, The Oona King Diaries*, London: Bloomsbury, 2007.

Klein, Emma, *The Battle for Auschwitz*, London, Portland, OR: Vallentine Mitchell, 2001.

Langham, Raphael, *The Jews in Britain*, New York: Palgrave Macmillan, 2005.

Laqueur, Walter, *The Changing Face of Anti-Semitism*, Oxford University Press, 2006.

LeBor, Adam, *City of Oranges: Arabs and Jews in Jaffa*, London: Bloomsbury, 2006.

Lebzelter, Gisela C., *Political Anti-Semitism in England 1918-1939*, London: Macmillan, 1978.

Lewis, Bernard, *Semites and Anti-Semites: An Inquiry into Conflict and Prejudice*, London: Phoenix, 1997.

Lineham, Thomas, *British Fascism 1918-1939: Parties, Ideology and Culture*, Manchester: Manchester University Press, 2000.

Lipman, V.D., *A History of the Jews in Britain since 1858*, Leicester: Leicester University Press, 1990.

London, Louise, *Whitehall and the Jews 1933-1948: British Immigration Policy, Jewish Refugees and the Holocaust*, Cambridge: Cambridge University Press, 2000.

Mearsheimer John J. and Walt Stephen M., *The Israel Lobby and US Foreign Policy*, New York: Farrar, Straus and Giroux, 2007.

Meddeb, Abdelwahab, *Sortir de la malediction: L'islam entre civilisation et barbarie*, Paris: Seuil, 2008

Mende, Tibor, *De l'aide à la recolonisation*, France: Seuil, 1975.

Menocal, María Rosa, *Ornament of the World*, New York, Boston: Little, Brown and Company, 2002.

Merkel, Peter H. and Weinberg Leonard, eds., *The Revival of Right-wing Extremism in the Nineties*, London: Frank Cass, 1997.

Morin, Edgar, *Le monde moderne et la question juive*, Paris: Seuil, 2006.

Mosse, Werner E., ed. *Second Chance: Two Centuries of German-Speaking Jews in the United Kingdom*, Tübingen: Mohr, 1991.

O'Brien, Conor Cruise, *The Siege*, London: Weidenfeld & Nicolson, 1986.

Parkes, James, *The Emergence of the Jewish Problem 1878-1939*, London: Oxford University Press, 1946.

Patten, Chris, *Not Quite the Diplomat: Home Truths About World Affairs*, London: Allen Lane, Penguin Books, 2005.

Phillips, Melanie, *Londonistan*, London: Gibson Square, 2006.

Poliakov, Léon, *Histoire de l'antisémitisme*, 1: *L'âge de la foi*, Paris: Calmann-Lévy, 1981.

Poliakov, Léon, *Histoire de l'antisémitisme*, 2: *L'âge de la science*, Paris: Calmann-Lévy, 1981.

Poliakov, Léon, *The History of Anti-Semitism*, Vol. IV: *Suicidal Europe 1870-1933*, Oxford: Oxford University Press, 1985.

Prior, Michael, *Zionism and the State of Israel, A Moral Inquiry*, London: Routledge, 1999.

Raphael, Frederic, *The Necessity of Anti-Semitism*, Manchester: Carcanet, 1997.

Roxburgh, Angus, *Preachers of Hate: The Rise of the Far Right*, London: Gibson Square, 2002.

Roy, Olivier, *Secularism Confronts Islam*, New York: Columbia University Press, 2007.

Roy, Olivier, *Le croissant et le chaos*, Paris: Hachette Littératures, 2007.

Rubinstein, W.D., *A History of the Jews in the English-Speaking World*, London: Macmillan, 1996.

Ruthven, Malise, *A Satanic Affair: Salman Rushdie and the Wrath of Islam*, London: Hogarth Press, 1990.

Saad-Ghorayeb, Amal, *Hizbu'llah*, London: Pluto, 2002.

Sassoon, Donald, *The Culture of the Europeans - From 1800 to the Present*, London: HarperCollins, 2006.

Sen, Amartya, *Identity and Violence: The Illusion of Destiny*, London: Penguin, 2006.

Stephens, Robert, *Political Leaders of the Twentieth Century: Nasser*, England: Penguin Books, 1973.

Sterman, Lionel B., *Paths to Genocide: Antisemitism in Western History*, London: Macmillan, 1998.

Sternhell, Zeev, *The Founding Myths of Israel*, Princeton, New Jersey: Princeton University Press, 1998.

Taguieff, Pierre-André, *L'Imaginaire du Complot Mondial*, Paris: Mille et Une Nuits, 2006.

Thurlow, Richard C., *Fascism in Modern Britain*, England: Sutton Publishing, 2000.

Select Bibliography

Vidal-Naquet Pierre, *Les assassins de la mémoire*, Paris: La Découverte, 2005.

Waitzfelder, Monica, *L'Oréal Took My Home: The Secrets of a Theft*, London: Arcadia, 2008.

Weber, Eugen, *My France: Politics-Culture-Myths*, Cambridge, Mass.: Harvard University Press, 1991.

Wheatcroft, Geoffrey, *The Controversy of Zion*, Harlow, England: Addison-Wesley Publishing Company, 1996.

Wieviorka, Michel, *La tentation anti-Sémite*, Paris: Laffont, 2005.

Winock Michel, *Nationalisme, antisémitisme et fascisme en France*, Paris: Seuil, 2004.

Wistrich, Robert S., *Anti-Semitism: The Longest Hatred*, London: Thames Methuen, 1991.

Index

Index